Lake

Lake

Old Raven nest (abandoned)

Cliff

Lake

enwood

The "tch"

Raven encounter

Cliff

Cascade

Winter

Beaver dam

Bush

Camp

Wolves kill deer

Raven Eye

Mink Rocks

Beaver Lodge

Animal Trail

Beaver Lodge

High Pond

Winter

Wolf packs battle

Lake

4 wolves chase deer

ves hunt beaver

Cliff overlook

Blueberry Hill

Winter

Old prospectors Cabin

Otter slide

reek

Beaver Valley

Wolves kill deer

Large White pines

Lake

Troll Island

Winter

Fox den

Otter slide

Beaver dam

Big Bog

Nothern Light Island

Moose Pond

ow

Spruce bog

Winter

Bush Camp

Black

Wolf

Mwooky Land

Angry Bull Moose

Giant White-tail Buck

Wolf Encounter
Wolf Kill
Foot Trail

BROTHER WOLF

A Forgotten Promise

Brother Wolf: A Forgotten Promise

Jim Brandenburg

NorthWord Press, Inc.

For my beloved pack members, Heidi, Anthony, and Judy.

DEDICATION

COWLES
Creative Publishing, Inc.

Cowles Creative Publishing, Inc.
5900 Green Oak Drive
Minnetonka, Minnesota 55343
1-800-328-3895

Editor-in-chief: Greg Linder
Production Coordinator: Russell S. Kuepper
Text edited by Michael Furtman

Book design and concept: Ravenwood Studio and
Little & Company, Minneapolis, MN

Illustrations: Jack Molloy

Hand Lettering: Julian Waters

Printed in Singapore

Kodak photo CD and digital imaging and retouching performed
on a Macintosh Quadra 950 at Ravenwood Studios.

The author will contribute a portion of the proceeds
from this book to Wolf Ridge Environmental Learning
Center, Defenders of Wildlife and other groups involved
in wolf protection and education.

Library of Congress Number 93-19651   ISBN 1-55971-210-4

Table of Contents

I first must thank Michael Furtman, whose empathy for the essential wildness of wolves and whose understanding of nature's primal forces made him invaluable in helping to fashion the text of *Brother Wolf*. When I had a personal experience that was not yet a story, Mike helped me organize my thoughts for the printed page. I thank him for his skills, his sensitivity, and his contribution.

Special thanks to:

Dick Hall, who for ten years has diligently watched over Ravenwood during my absences, ensuring that it remained "wolf-friendly." *Brother Wolf* would not have been possible without him.

Andy Baugnet, who has recently brought new enthusiasm and a higher degree of organization to Ravenwood Studios.

Anthony, Heidi and Judy Brandenburg for their endless help and support with this project.

Tom and Pat Klein, my publishers, for sticking with me through the difficulties and challenges of *White Wolf* and now *Brother Wolf*.

ACKNOWLEDGMENTS

Dave Peterson at Watt-Peterson, Inc., for his interest in the project, his commitment to quality, and his technological assistance in linking Ravenwood Studios' photo CD digital computer technology with state-of-the-art printing processes.

Larry Minden, Ray Pfortner, Chris Carey and Stacy Frank at Minden Pictures, my agency in Aptos, CA, that keeps exceptional track of all my photographs.

Karen Geiger, who incorporated my design ideas into *Brother Wolf* and went beyond the call of duty in monitoring the progress of the design to its completion.

And to those who have given me moral and technical support, I am deeply grateful: Lori Schmidt; Paula Berglund; Vic Van Ballenberghe; Paul Pacquet, Paul Winter and Chez Liley; Diane Neimann; Greg Linder and Russ Kuepper from NorthWord Press; Jack Pichotta at Wolf Ridge; Don and Val Beland; Jeff Hway; Deborah Warrick; Diane Wolfgram; Sandy Bridges; Bob and Lil Carey; Bob and Edith Sommer; Rod Sando; Al Heidebrink; Glenn Maxham; Rodger Schlickeisen; Bill Graves; Mike Link; James Taylor; Steve Werner; Larry, Paisley, Chinook and Sam; and to the many other friends and family who are too numerous to mention, your loyalty and support is not forgotten.

Fate has been good to me.

For most of my adult life I've been able to travel the world widely, photographing wildlife in some of the most spectacular settings imaginable.

Part of that job is waiting—waiting for the sun to shine, waiting for the animals to appear, waiting, even, in airports. This time to myself has not been spent idly. Seeing the wonders of nature has spurred me to contemplate its intricacies and how our race relates to this finely tuned organism.

What you are about to read is part of that mental wandering. It is not science. Some of it even contradicts science. But I hope I bring to the realm of nature study and, in this case, to our newfound appreciation for the wolf, a perspective that complements science, and is just as valid.

The wolves of Ellesmere Island, chronicled in my previous book, *White Wolf*, showed me the full range of wolf behavior. Studying wolves in the forests of Minnesota is a much more difficult task, for here they are much more secretive. In creating *Brother Wolf*, I relied upon the cooperation of the wild wolves near my Ravenwood retreat, but I also included a few photos of research wolves or others acclimated to human presence. All of the photos accurately depict wolf behavior.

If the questions I raise in my meandering with wolves cause you to ask even more questions about our relationship with them, I'll consider the long hours I spent alone worth the effort.

Jim Brandenburg

To My Readers . . .

Foreword by Canis Lupus

Since only the sun and moon made light, I have known you. I watched you from the once vast, impenetrable forest. I was witness as you discovered fire and strange tools. From ridges, I watched you hunt, and envied your kills. I have eaten your scraps. You have eaten mine.

I have heard your songs and watched your dancing shadows around bright fires. In a time so distant that I can barely remember, some of us joined you to sit near those fires. We became part of your packs, joined in your hunts, protected your pups, helped you, feared you, loved you.

We have existed together a long time. We were much alike. It is why the tame ones adopted you. Some of you, I know, respected me, the wild one. I am a good hunter. I respected you, too. You were a good hunter. I would see you hunt in a pack with the tame ones and catch meat.

Then there was always plenty. Then there were few of you. Then the woods was big. We howled to the tame ones in the night. Some came back to hunt with us. Some we ate, for they had become very strange. It was this way for a long long time. It was a good way.

Sometimes I would steal from you, as you did from me. Do you remember when you were starving and the snow was deep and you ate the meat we killed? It was a game. It was a debt. Some might call it a promise.

Like many of the tame ones, most of you have become very strange. Now I do not recognize some of the tame ones. Now I do not recognize some of you. We were once so much alike. You made the meat tame, too. When I began to hunt your tame meat (they are foolish creatures and do not honor death, but the wild meat was gone), you hunted me. I do not understand. When your packs grew larger and fought among themselves, I saw. I watched your great battles. I feasted on those you left behind. Then you hunted me more. I do not understand. They were meat. You killed them.

We wild ones are now very few. You made the woods small. You have killed many of us. But I still hunt, and I feed our hidden pups. I always will. I wonder if the tame ones who live with you made a good choice. They have lost the spirit to live in the wild. They are many, but they are strange. We are few. I still watch you, too, so I can avoid you.

I do not think I know you any longer.

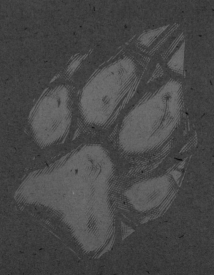

INTRODUCTION

I believe I felt the shadow even before I awoke. A renting beak and four-foot wings swept over, and it eyed me as a meal while I lay in the September sun, high atop a granite cliff. When the great bird yelped a piercing yell, I came fully awake but lay motionless, with one arm still cast over my eyes.

The raven called again. Although I did not know it at the time, this call was not one of friendship, or even one of curiosity. As it called, the raven sought the help of wolves to rip this new carcass it had spotted, and to open my body to its prying beak.

I watched from sheltered eyes. The wise black bird cautiously flew to a bony limb of a twisted jackpine. It studied me, glossy head cocked to one side, black liquid eye riveted on me. For what seemed an eternity I remained still, fascinated by the prospect of the bird moving closer. Occasionally the raven repeated its yell, trying to recruit other ravens or its partner, the wolf.

Gliding down with a barely audible whoosh, the raven flew to me atop my stony perch, landing just yards away, hopping as though the granite was too hot to stand on. It was as if the bird was goading me to move, testing to see what I would do. I remained frozen.

Around and below us swept the vast Minnesota forest, hills and valleys filled with splendid autumn aspen gold. Blood-red maples punctuated the landscape. Spruce and pine contrasted darkly with the quivering aspens and birch. And above, the blue sky was filled with the raucous talk of the serious raven.

Doing its ritual dance, the raven darted in and out, as if drawn to me but unsure. I could hardly contain my excitement at being so courted, though I might not have been so thrilled if I had known the raven's wishes. Stiff-legged, the raven worked cautiously toward me, seeming annoyed at the lack of response to its calls for help, and convinced now that I wouldn't move.

Cramped, and with an appointment waiting for me back at my cabin, I rose slowly to one elbow and faced my company. Intelligent and cautious birds, ravens are seldom caught this unaware or approached so near. If I was surprised by my good luck, the raven was flabbergasted that I had suddenly moved. If one can read the emotion in a raven's eyes, I swear this one felt bewildered by the rising of my once-prone body. I've come to believe since that the bird assumed I was a corpse.

As the rattled raven flew off, I trotted down the slope and onto the cool, wooded trail below, and began my walk back to the cabin. My ears were ringing and buzzing with the excitement of the encounter. Hovering above, sometimes flitting from tree to tree, the raven followed. Maybe it was waiting, hoping that I would keel over. At the time, however, I thought perhaps this was a sign of friendship. Honored, I felt I had finally found a name for my cabin-in-the-woods photography base: Ravenwood.

I've since come to understand, however, that ravens are much more interested in carcasses than company.

Ravenwood is my sanctuary, tucked in the wilds of northern Minnesota. It represents my cathedral, my dream, my sanity. I come here to work and think, and it is very cherished for all of that, but more so because it is a

place where wolves live. It has been my private challenge to get to know these wolves and the land on which they live.

Somehow my two long fascinations—my study of wolves and wild canids (dog-like animals), and my yearning for the great northwoods—seem linked in a way transcending the obvious fact that wolves live within the forest. The connection, I believe, has to do with the northwoods being alive because of the wolves. Like mountains without grizzlies, forests without wolves seem empty.

I didn't always know this, but I seemed continually to be in the process of learning it. My fantasy from childhood was a cabin in the tall pines in some northern place. The cabin would be built of logs and topped with a chimney. Smoke would curl from the chimney, spiraling through the reaching, soughing pine boughs, and the air would be so cold it would sting.

You have to understand that I grew up in southwestern Minnesota, near the town of Luverne. This is corn country, and it was once a land of expansive prairies. Little or no prairie could be found when I was a boy, even less today, and although young, I sensed something lacking. The works of people lay everywhere on the land, and the works were a burden to it. In Minnesota, the land of 10,000 lakes, I was somehow living in the only county without one.

But there were trips to the north! Our family migrated each summer to rented cabins on Lake Winnibegoshish, to troll for marble-eyed walleyes. Wild enough even today to hold wolves, the north was wilder then, and it was where the lure of the mysterious wilderness first tempted me.

I found the dragging of fishing lures boring, though the eating of walleye was delightful, and I beseeched my father to leave me ashore to explore. Looking back at it from a distance of years, I am quite sure my father was chagrined by this. His little boy wanted to catch frogs, watch birds and butterflies, and walk in the woods, not go fishing with his old dad. But my parents have always encouraged me, and these occasions were no different. They sometimes consented to leave me ashore. I was free to explore.

I don't remember how old I was the first time I timidly approached the forest. Certainly not old enough to be alone, so I'm sure someone must have been watching me. But I do remember the sandy soil and the game trails that led me into the woods. I do remember the forest beckoning and being drawn into it. And I vividly remember the heady scent of pine in the warm summer air, so very intoxicating to a farm boy accustomed to dust. With every step I took into the forest, I felt as if I was entering a fairy tale. I looked at the animal tracks in the sandy path. I touched the exotic plants. I started to picture the small animals and deer that had made the tracks. And then I felt it. Something was out there. Something mysterious and powerful. Something old. Part of me wanted to go deeper and deeper.

Part of me still does.

If those early trips enamored me with the northwoods, my experiences in farm country during my teens galvanized my fascination with canid predators.

In those days I was a hunter, and I still feel that learning the skills of the stalk was crucial to my development as a wildlife photographer and naturalist.

Though I pursue wildlife now with a camera, I've always considered myself a hunter of sorts, even though I last hunted with a gun as a 17-year-old, 30 years ago.

It was on these early hunting trips that I first learned to appreciate nature. To this day, tracking animals in the morning after a fresh snow is a passion, born of those early days afield. It was on these early excursions that I first met the wild canids.

One morning when I was probably about 14, while looking for gophers in a nearby pasture, I startled a red fox. The country there is nearly flat, but through this pasture the Rock River had cut its gentle course, leaving a rolling valley. I loved that place for its hills, so unusual on the prairie, behind which a young boy could imagine a world not of cornfields, but of prairie, buffalo, and Indians. The hills concealed reality, allowing me to envision a world long gone, a world without silos and barns.

If I close my eyes today, I can still see the startled fox loping gracefully up the hill across from me, parting the dewy grass, its red tail a bright plume in the morning light.

I stood stunned by the sight, captivated by the thought of this wild "dog" living here, right here, in a world so wrought by humans. When you are a young adventurer, the very notion of living off the land sends chills down your skinny back. Here was an animal doing just that, and it struck me as magical. Mostly, if we thought of animals at all around here, we thought of pheasants and cows. This was different. The fox was a predator, higher up the ladder. It dawned on me then that the fox and I had been sharing the same pasture, and even the same activity.

From that day on, I was hooked on foxes. I skipped school to track them, study them, hunt and trap them. I was a fanatic, often following a set of tracks through new snow for miles and hours, in the hope of just seeing the fox. There was always the thrill of reading how it lived by interpreting its tracks; seeing where it had slept, and where it had caught the pheasant.

One day I stumbled upon something even more wonderful than a fox. A coyote! In all my explorations, I had never seen one before. In those days in our county, a coyote was almost unheard of, so my experience even made the newspaper. More importantly, seeing the coyote fueled my fascination with wild canids. Here was a bigger, more wily predator than I had imagined, another dog-like animal. My thoughts turned to coyotes and then, inevitably, to their near relative, the wolf.

I suppose I knew then that there were wolves in Minnesota. But I don't remember thinking about them until after my meeting with the coyote. Since the first time I imagined the greatest of canids prowling the woods, they have also prowled my mind.

Now I had one more element to add to my fantasy of the cabin in the pines: the wolf.

Canis lupus, the wolf of my imagination and of the northern forest, did indeed roam Minnesota. Once the most abundant large predator on the continent, the wolf had virtually been eliminated from most places. Minnesota remained the only state among the lower 48 where a truly viable population existed.

The still-untracked wilderness in the northeast part of the state provided a reprise for the eastern grey wolf, or timber wolf. With moose and deer available as major prey and an abundance of another favorite food, beaver, the wolf stalked this forest. It was bountied still and often trapped. But the forest was large, and wolves were smart, so they held on in virtual secrecy.

A highly intelligent and social animal, this apex predator lives in small family units of about six animals. Generally, each group is dominated by the alpha male and female, which are also usually the pack's only breeding pair. Juveniles, from this year's pups to teenagers, generally make up the rest of the group, with an occasional ousted alpha elder hanging on. The pack focuses on hunting communally, a strategy that allows the killing of large prey, and caring for the pups, which are their future. Because in most cases only one pair breeds per pack, every wolf takes some part in the caring for, defending, and feeding of the young. Food sharing is common. Leaders remain leaders only as long as they function well. It is a social system and hunting strategy so successful that the wolf has flourished wherever it roamed. One other highly intelligent predator either mimicked it or evolved along the same lines.

That predator is us.

In my work for the National Geographic Society, I have traveled the world. I have photographed exotic places and creatures, met fascinating people, and experienced cultures ranging from the most "sophisticated" to the most "primitive."

Three threads have run continually through my life.

I thought often of wolves. They were both a professional and personal challenge.

I never forgot my dream of the northwoods cabin. Embodied in this dream was a yearning to get to know a piece of land as intimately as one knows a lover.

Lastly, I constantly envisioned a world that appeared unscarred by man, a world as it might have looked before humans became so numerous and destructive. I tried to capture this world in every photograph I took.

All three were coming together as I reached my middle years. The raven had welcomed me to my newly acquired acres in the northwoods, and had helped me name them. My cabin awaited beneath the Norway pines at the end of the path, and I could smell the wood smoke as I walked back.

And in the wilderness surrounding Ravenwood, wolves lived as wolves have always lived. The forest crackled with their primal energy. The nights were alive with their singing.

Only the last thread remained: to find and photograph these mysterious animals in the dense forest. As I had when I was a child, I followed the path. Something was out there. Something mysterious and powerful. Something old. I knew then it was the wolf.

Now I could go deeper and deeper.

A RAVENWOOD WOLF—AS ELUSIVE AS A SHADOW.

WOLVES AND RAVENWOOD

tartled in the near-dark, I turned at the noise. Over the hump of the cabin driveway, two animals charged toward me. Caught unaware and feeling enormously vulnerable, I froze next to the half-built cabin, where I had been working in the dusk. There was no time to react. The forms became more distinct as they approached. A lump of alarm and wonder lodged where my Adam's apple should have been. Lynx?

Wolves!

If we retain any instincts from our ancestors, it is the fight-or-flight response, which sends adrenaline pumping. I could feel my body charged, taut. Then a smile split my face, and a chuckle replaced the lump in my throat. The two "ferocious" killers charging me were half-grown wolf pups. When they spotted me, they skidded to a stop in a whirl of fur on puppy-paw brakes.

Anyone who has had the good fortune of watching wolves is amazed by their similarity to our dogs. These two naive wolf pups watched me for a moment, sheepishly tucking their tails between their legs, ears flat, eyes puzzled. Then,

like our puppies with their short attention spans, the wolf pups forgot about me and began to romp and play—the very same play that dogs exhibit. Up and down they raced, tugging on each other, leaping over each other's backs, growling puppy growls with their butts up and their heads on the ground.

While I was watching the nipping, rolling, wolf-pup fur ball bounce around my driveway in the fading light, another actor silently entered the scene. I don't know how long it had been standing there, but when I heard a squeak and looked up the hill, I saw another wolf outlined against the dark sky. This animal was an adult, and it paced nervously back and forth at the edge of the forest, no more than ten yards from me. It was obviously concerned about the safety of the pups that continued to romp before me.

I was amazed at the range of nervous squeaks the adult emitted in its attempt to get the puppies' attention. Whether it was the mother or another adult in charge of baby-sitting, I'll never know. But the wolf's distress at failing in its duties was evident in its voice. Though I was much too near the pups for the adult's liking, it made no threatening sounds or motions. In fact, its response to me was quite the opposite. It merely wanted to call the pups away without causing a scene.

As I kept an eye on the pups and the adult, I moved cautiously to the place where my gear was stored and searched for a camera. Cameras I had, and lots of film, too, but I was chagrined to discover that I didn't have a flash unit. Crushed, I instead grabbed a tape recorder and moved quietly back to the pups, wanting to at least capture the sounds. The nearly frantic adult was now pacing and imploring the pups to come to it. I howled at the wolf and it howled back to me, filling the night with its electricity. We talked back and forth, though I don't know what we said.

Exciting? Short of my work with the white arctic wolves of Ellesmere Island, this was by far the most intimate encounter I'd ever had with wolves. I was thrilled. I was also angry and frustrated. Here I was, the globe-trotting photographer, caught without a flash unit. My frustration was palpable.

The whole play lasted ten or fifteen minutes. I relaxed as the pups continued their romp, and I was flattered that they seemed to trust me. Then, like dog puppies, the wolf pups wearied. And like a dog that abruptly "recovers" its hearing after being called repeatedly, the pups now responded to the imploring adult. On oversized puppy paws, the pair scrambled up the hill to the adult, and the three wolves disappeared into the night.

I could almost hear the adult's sigh of relief.

That first incident with wolves at Ravenwood went a long way toward convincing me that I had made a good choice when I selected the area for my wolf work. I knew I needed to be in a place that was still very wild, but I also knew I needed a home base.

A LONE WOLF STAYS IN TOUCH WITH ITS PACK.

twenty-one

RAVENWOOD'S BACKYARD: THE BOUNDARY WATERS WILDERNESS.

twenty-four

Wildlife photography is always arduous work. It is sometimes lonely, and it is always intense. But some animals can be captured on film much easier than others. Some animals congregate in numbers at certain places and certain times. Others are not particularly skittish, and more easily tolerate a photographer. But wolves present a particular set of problems, which is why most wolf photography is done with captive wolf packs placed in natural settings.

Wolves are too rare to stumble onto, and they're too wary to be fooled by common photographer tricks. Timber wolves are hidden by the cover of trees. Even glimpses of them are rare. They're secretive and mysterious, and their story is often revealed only through tracks in the snow. But it was my passion, or perhaps my obsession, to photograph wolves in the woods, so I had long thought about how to tell their story.

Considering the size of a wolf pack's range and the slight odds of actually encountering them within that range, I knew I had to devise another method. Years ago, I had spent the better part of the winter in the Minnesota wilderness, in an abortive attempt to photograph wolves. Even with the support of the U.S. Forest Service, which had flown me and my two months' worth of camping supplies into a territory where three packs roamed, I was unable to produce even one bad photograph, let alone tell their story. That particular approach was prone to failure. But a new method had since been forming in my mind.

Thankfully, Ravenwood was located in wolf country, and the happenstance of the wolf pups indicated that I was on the right track. I had decided that the best approach would involve placing myself in the wolves' path, so to speak, as they made the rounds of their territory. With time, patience, and a good slice of luck, I ought to find myself in the right place from time to time. And I've always believed that you make your own luck through hard work. Ravenwood just might be the tool to help pull it off.

The land surrounding Ravenwood is some of the grandest country in the world. Northeastern Minnesota lies atop the Canadian shield, that vast granite underpinning of eastern North America. Repeatedly scraped and carved by the ebb and flow of glaciers, the earth was stripped to this ancient crust as the last glacier retreated some 12,000 years ago. It is stony, bony country, with rock ridges and primordial bogs. The forest is thick, tangled, and immense. But one thing makes it penetrable. It is lake country.

Thousands of lakes, linked by dozens of rivers, sparkle across the landscape and are the melted carcasses of the glacier. These waterways, whether navigated by canoe in the summer or crossed when frozen in the long winter, make travel possible.

The hills and valleys are covered with boreal forest. Dark pines, spruce, and fir spire toward the sky. Aspen, birch, and maple add their leafed diversity. Moose roam the woodland. At one time, not so very long ago, woodland caribou fed in the jackpine forest and galloped across frozen lakes. And

after timber barons built America and lined their pockets by stripping this area of its tall pines, the second-growth forest attracted white-tailed deer.

Undoubtedly, wolves have been part of the region since this area was barely more than a rocky tundra growing in the wake of the slowly receding glacier. We know from archaeological sites that ancient humans, the Paleo-Indians, followed herds of caribou found here at the time. It seems almost certain that wolves, the most successful mammal (next to us) in the world, also feasted on that caribou flesh. As the land evolved into forest during the warmer ages that followed, wolves adapted too, stalking moose in the white winters and catching beavers in the green summers.

Though more than half of the virgin forest has been logged and the caribou are gone, the land surrounding Ravenwood represents the last vestiges of the once seemingly endless eastern forest. Just to the north of my land, along the Minnesota-Ontario border, lies the Boundary Waters Canoe Area Wilderness, about one million acres of federally protected forest. Abutting the Boundary Waters on the Canadian side is another million acres of protected wilderness, Quetico Provincial Park. If a line was drawn on a map between Ravenwood and the North Pole, it would cross only two major east-west roads.

The thought of all that wilderness between me and the Arctic thrills and comforts me. Just as the boy had imagined the prairie as it was before the coming of European settlers, the man needs to know that wilderness survives despite the contemporary epidemic of development.

Wolves have survived here. With a buffer of wilderness clear to the Arctic, the genetic artery of wildlife is not severed, but functions well because of

this northerly reserve. It is entirely possible that there are more wolves in this region now than were here a hundred years ago. The newcomer white-tailed deer is probably more numerous than the caribou were, especially in the areas south and west of the protected wilderness, where periodic logging creates the young forest habitat needed by whitetails. Since wolves don't much care what kind of venison they eat, they've done well by switching from one kind of deer to the other. And when the prey base grew, so did the number of wolves.

Other factors contributed, of course. Wolves in Minnesota have been as persecuted and vilified as wolves elsewhere. A bounty on wolves existed as recently as 1965. They were classified as an endangered species in 1966, and it wasn't until 1974 that they were fully protected. At that time, around 1,000 wolves roamed the Minnesota forest. Recent surveys indicate that perhaps as many as 2,000 now hunt the northern forest, and their range has expanded to the south and west, proof that they've responded well to the protection granted them.

My good fortune in acquiring Ravenwood was coincidentally timed with the increase in wolf numbers. And since the animals hadn't been trapped or bountied for over 20 years, I believe they had less fear of humans, making them more approachable.

All of which was in my favor. Years ago, when I was still in college, I asked wolf researcher Milt Stenlund of the Minnesota Department of Natural Resources how I might go about photographing wolves. His answer was polite and professional, but now that much of my naiveté has worn away, I can see that he was trying to be honest without bursting my bubble. It now seems clear that he thought my quest was impossible. He told me that good

woodsmen had spent a lifetime in wolf country but caught only a glimpse or two of wolves, and that I shouldn't get my hopes up. Though I may not have sensed the full range of his skepticism, I did sense some.

At the time, his cautionary words made me that much more determined. The more I thought about how difficult my task would be, the more I felt challenged. Part of me has always wanted to disprove doubters, even though a part of me has always doubted, too. I began to believe that I had at least a small chance of success.

The site for my Ravenwood cabin was chosen after much hiking and searching. I wanted a location that did not disrupt the functioning of the land and its wildlife, yet I needed to be at a spot where animals would be funneled to me.

A small creek flows on the property. Most of the time, it winds its way quietly through bogs and forest, heading north and west to one of the area's larger lakes. From there, the water eventually flows west through the length of the Boundary Waters, from lakes to rivers to lakes, then on through Voyageurs National Park and the Rainy Lake watershed. Still farther, it turns north once more and flows to Lake Winnipeg, mingles with the waters of a thousand other such creeks, and finally dumps into Hudson Bay.

I doubt whether, along any part of its journey, the water of this creek passes through a spot as charming as the one where I chose to build. After hastening down a little rapids, the creek leaps over a 20-foot waterfall, splashing noisily into the dark bowl below. Along the bank nearby, I found the beds of two

Two elusive yet social creatures share a remarkable symbiotic relationship. The raven, mobile and intelligent, observes from the sky, then appears to summon the wolf to hunt a vulnerable animal such as a weakened moose or whitetail, or to open a carcass. These are two of the most intelligent animals in North America. Are they, too, partners in an ancient covenant?

My ravenwood cabin on the creek.

moose as I scouted my new land. I chose to build where the moose had slept, contouring the cabin into the hill stair-step fashion, rather than flattening the land and imposing my cabin upon it. Here I would always have the beauty of the falls and the comfort of its rumble. It would drown out human noises and camera clicks as I recorded the animal life around me.

In positioning the cabin, there was a serious consideration other than aesthetics. Creeks and rivers carve corridors, along which wildlife travel. If prey travels through, so, eventually, will wolves. Additionally, a rock outcrop sits across the tiny valley of the creek, beneath towering white and Norway pines. By occasionally dragging road-killed animals to this spot, I hoped to encourage wolves to pause during their travels. I would do this sporadically, only in the winter, and often separated by months, for I did not want to condition the wolves to feeding here all the time, like garbage-dump bears. But if the wolves whose territory included Ravenwood found food here once in a while, they would remember. They might stop by when they passed through, especially if they felt safe on my land. When they did appear, I could photograph them through the special optical glass windows I had strategically placed in the cabin.

Eventually I would spend many hours, sniper-like, behind camouflage cabin curtains, waiting for the wolves. For days on end, I would be afraid to venture outside, fearing that I would drive the wolves away. But once they felt safe near the cabin and had become accustomed to my presence, I hoped, too, that they would tolerate me as I followed them into the forest. Getting

them used to the cabin area would make picking up their tracks an easier task, and once I had determined how and where they traveled, my prospects for studying them away from the artifice of the cabin would increase.

I didn't really expect other wolves to be as trusting as the pups. But with good fortune, I'd finally be able to observe and photograph the wolves of the northwoods, just as I had photographed the white wolves of the Arctic.

In 1981, I was commissioned by the U.S. Postal Service to design ten postage stamps. I was to select and photograph ten animals, all of which were prominent and popular megafauna such as bears and bighorn sheep. When I delivered the designs, nine were greeted with warmth and enthusiasm. One was greeted with icy disgust. It portrayed a wolf.

Deep within the den of bureaucratic offices in Washington, D.C., I was told in no uncertain terms that a postage stamp depicting such a "negative" animal would be too controversial. The Postal Service, they said, wanted nothing to do with promoting the wolf. The design was rejected, and I was instructed to come up with something less objectionable. I barely met the requirements the second time by submitting another bloodthirsty killer, the mountain lion.

It was strange to me. The American public had by that time begun embracing the environment. People were concerned about protecting some species. They supported the protection of wilderness areas. Perhaps the Postal Service

THE CABIN'S WOODEN WOLF ALWAYS RUNS INTO THE WIND.

A BLACK-PHASE, KNOWN LOCALLY AS A SIBERIAN WOLF.

thirty-four

merely reflected the attitude held by many at the time (and by some today): Protect the pretty animals. Protect the trees and scenery. Nature, after all, is benign. Nature is a theme park. Nature is peaceful and non-violent. Any animal that disturbs the serenity of the theme park must be a very bad animal.

Yet predators stalk through those protected wildernesses. They hunt and kill. There is violence and death, but it is neither senseless nor meaningless. Protecting the environment means protecting this process as well. And in the creation of life from death lies the true function of nature.

But we fear death, and so animals that inflict it must be evil. I doubt that Postal Service officials thought it through at great length, but I do *not* doubt that our long indoctrination of fear was the subconscious basis for their decision. The time of the wolf had not come. Yes, it was protected. But it wasn't embraced. And there's a further irony here: Unlike the wolf, the mountain lion has on numerous occasions stalked and killed human beings.

To fear and hate those wolf pups would have been wrong. I knew that, and I have always known that. The pups' simple truth was this: They would grow up and eat deer. They need not apologize for that, any more than I should. I wanted to go into the woods not as a dispassionate scientist to measure teeth and tracks and examine scat, but as an entirely passionate observer. I wanted to know this land, see how it functioned, learn of the wolf's role. You can not do that without passion, for in wilderness is truth, and the truth of nature is full of passion, is all about chase and evasion, capture and death, blood and birth. If we fear these things, then it is no wonder we have long feared the wolf. It is nature's truth. It is our truth.

The time of the wolf had finally come.

TURKEY VULTURES AWAIT THEIR TURN AT A KILL.

WOLF: THE HUNTER

W orking on snowshoes under a full load of gear, I savored the first huffs and puffs of frigid wilderness air as I eased into an animal rhythm, my empty car a

speck behind me on the shore of frozen Kawishiwi Lake.

Immersing myself in the Minnesota wilderness again, following tracks in the fresh snow, was more than just an enjoyable pastime. When I hunkered over fresh tracks, something deep inside me stirred, an old sense, a reflection of some ancient past bigger and older than me, a part of my race's memory. I slipped quickly into the intensity of that past.

Throughout the day, I encountered wolf tracks. I saw tracks on the portage trails and others on frozen lakes. Some tracks were old and barely discernible in the drifted snow. Others were fresh—large pad marks on the white Minnesota landscape, telling tales of travels and hunts, mystery and excitement. Each time I rounded a bend in the trail or stepped from the forest onto the bright plain of a frozen lake, I hesitated, hoping to glimpse the makers of the tracks. Above the hiss of snowshoes on the snow and the creaking of bindings, my senses were fully alive, intent upon seeing, hearing, finding wolves.

Miles were eaten during the day. The more miles behind me, the more wolf sign before me. It was a good omen. I decided to make my winter camp among the dark conifers that offered protection from the wind and shelter from any snow that might fall.

My back hurt. I shifted the backpack to release the straps that had been weighing for too long in one place, shrugging and rolling my shoulders to move blood into spots that had been too long without circulation. Arching my back, I looked for the sun in the sullied-cotton winter sky.

The day was drab, grey, and cold, and there was only an hour of daylight left—scarcely enough time to make a camp. As the sub-zero temperatures began to penetrate my sweat-dampened clothes, I shuffled toward the forest, looking for a sheltered place among the spruce and pines to spend the night.

Establishing a winter camp is a time-consuming affair, for doing anything at ten below zero takes extra care. Tents erect slowly, fingers freeze quickly, and zippers and buckles behave awkwardly. Cooking seems to take forever, and firewood must be gathered in quantity.

In the dusk, just as my tasks were nearly completed, they came. I could not see them in the darkness, but they were near. A chorus of wolf howls fractured the frigid air; I stood rigid with delight. I listened and tried to imagine them in the forest.

Close your eyes. See them? Their heads are back, eyes closed, muzzles angled up and slightly open, black lips parted. Their vaporous howls may be visible in the cold air. How many are there? It sounds as if the whole woods is alive with wolves. Surely there must be at least 10 or 15 in the pack.

Wolves have a wonderful talent for howling at different pitches. Each wolf assumes a unique pitch to avoid duplicating another pack member's voice. This ability gives humans and, I suspect, other wolf packs, the impression that many wolves are present. It especially confuses humans. Almost always, after hearing wolves howl, people tend to imagine a large pack. I am amazed by the wolf's talent, awed by nature's intricacy. In nature's demanding feint-and-challenge world, appearing to be larger or more numerous is always to an animal's advantage. To appear so through trickery of voice is wondrous.

The chorus continued for a few moments. As I stared into the dark west, in the direction of the sound, the wolves quit abruptly, leaving a lingering feeling of awe in my mind. I glanced at my watch. Only seven o'clock in the long winter night! Like a child who can barely stand waiting for Christmas morning, I anticipated the arrival of the distant dawn, when I could find and follow their tracks. The night would be excruciatingly long.

I was up early. Heading off to the west, I crossed the wolves' tracks within

minutes of leaving camp and followed their trail. Almost immediately, I came upon a spot where they had killed a moose. I paused, not wanting to disturb any of the evidence before me, curious about what had taken place here. I studied the wolf tracks carefully, and I could see that I must have surprised them while they were still cleaning the corpse. The tracks clearly showed that they had left in a hurry when they saw or heard me coming. Were they just beyond my sight, watching me?

My "woods full of wolves" turned out to be five animals, countable by the number of beds near the moose carcass. I turned my attention to the moose, or what was left of it. Except for the bones and the hide, it was completely eaten. I was impressed. A Minnesota moose weighs between 500 and 1,000 pounds, and the fact that five wolves could so completely consume one in so short a time was a gastronomical wonder—even though they may have been eating for several days, and possibly had the assistance of ravens.

As if it was being prepared for shipment to a museum, the moose skeleton remained virtually intact—ribs joined to spine, head joined to neck—but scarcely a sliver of meat was attached to any bone. The carcass would not have been cleaner if it had been dropped in the Amazon River and stripped by a cloud of piranha. Even the skin seemed nearly intact, appearing for all the world as though the wolves had peeled it off the moose. Completely boned, the hide was partially wrapped around a nearby tree.

The wolves of my dreams, though not yet seen, had finally become real. I had heard them, and I had visited the first of many kill sites I would examine in the coming years. They were so near that I could almost feel them.

Who knows what impresses you, what drives you to keep pursuing a dream?

Yearlings' first winter.

The answers to these questions are not always clear. But I know today that this first wolf experience was deeply motivational. Seeing the kill site was not an end to my ambition, but only stirred me, teased me. There were too many unanswered questions. How had they brought down this great beast? Had they chased it for a long time? Did they sense in it a vulnerability, a weakness that led to its demise?

For a moment, with closed eyes, I felt the excitement of the chase and the terror of the moose. I could hear the panting of the pack, the pounding of a thousand pounds across a frozen lake. Then, as a wolf clenched its jaws on the struggling moose, the two animals were joined, fused, one's life extended by the other's death; harm and harmony.

I opened my eyes and reached for my camera.

Look into the eyes of a wolf. In its yellow stare you will see, among other things, great intelligence. It is precisely that intelligence that makes the wolf a great hunter. And its great hunting ability has led humans first to admire, then to loathe, the wolf.

That intellect allowed wolves to adopt a social structure enabling them to hunt large animals. Only through cooperative hunting can the wolf success-fully attack and kill animals as large as the moose in Minnesota, or the musk-oxen on Ellesmere Island. The wolf of the great plains, now extinct, once made its living on the bison, the largest land mammal on the continent.

By contrast, the wolf's near relative, the coyote, rarely attempts to kill animals

PINE GROSBEAK

A CAUTIOUS COYOTE WATCHES FOR ITS LARGER COUSIN, THE WOLF.

larger than itself. Even a 150-pound white-tailed deer is fairly safe from coyotes (although there are exceptions, and coyotes do sometimes kill deer). The reason is quite simple. Coyotes generally hunt alone. I've seen them only infrequently in pairs. As a result, the coyote's prey must be of a size that one animal can handle. Nonetheless, the coyote fills its niche so successfully on this continent that it is expanding its range despite decades of predator control. Not only is the coyote skilled at finding small prey, it is skilled at avoiding humans.

The dire wolf, once common to this continent but extinct since the end of the last ice age (about 10,000 years ago), was a slightly larger, stockier wolf than the "true wolf" of today. It is thought that the dire wolf preyed primarily on large ice-age mammals, which also became extinct, and that neither the wolf nor its prey could evolve rapidly enough to adapt to the newer, warmer climate. The coyote and the dire wolf are genetically equidistant from the true wolf, and all existed simultaneously during the last period of glaciation, each within its own ecological niche.

Though no one really knows, scientists hypothesize that the dire wolf lacked the cooperative social structure of today's wolf, and therefore could not hunt the prey that wolves fed upon then and feed upon today. If so, it proves the adage that brains are superior to brawn. Though it is not a cooperative hunter, the coyote also possesses a swift intellect and has adapted well to today's world.

Of course, it is possible that the dire wolf is among us still, its genes absorbed by the grey wolf that flourished when the glaciers melted. Coyotes and wolves can interbreed, so it is possible that the dire wolf and true wolf interbred as the former declined and the latter spread. Today's Alaskan wolves, the largest in North America, are not much smaller than the dire wolf of the past.

The thought of interbreeding in the canid family scares some wolf supporters and researchers, for they fear that if an animal isn't all wolf (and thereby protected as an endangered species in many areas), it is a coyote, which can be freely killed. But to deny that mating between the two species occurs is to deny a potentially important aspect of nature's great flexibility. This is even more grist for the already dark and complicated "wolf politics" mill.

I believe that wolf-coyote hybrids occur occasionally wherever their two ranges overlap. I have seen animals that I initially have been unable to identify with certainty as either wolf or coyote—animals that seem to possess aspects of both. Those that confuse even experienced observers are the ones with characteristics of both species. There are animals that are clearly wolves, and there are coyotes that are unmistakable. But then . . .

Consider a young male wolf, ostracized for who knows what reason. Like humans who pick on a person who is "different," wolves sometimes drive individuals away from the pack. This young wolf, living alone, might encounter a female coyote in heat who, for reasons unknown to us, may be receptive to breeding with the wolf.

THE TRACKS, THE TRACKER, AND THE TRACKED.
WOLVES ARE PERPETUAL HUNTERS, BUT FOR
ALL THEIR STRENGTH AND SKILL, THEY
ARE OFTEN UNSUCCESSFUL. A HEALTHY
DEER—ALERT, SPEEDY, AND ELUSIVE—MOST
OFTEN ESCAPES. THESE HUNTS ARE THE
TIMELESS SURVIVAL TESTS OF NATURE:
THE STRONG SURVIVE, THE WEAK SUCCUMB.

Such matings are not farfetched. Wolf-dog and coyote-dog crosses are accepted occurrences. Until a few years ago, and perhaps still on occasion, Inuits purposely introduced wolf genes into their sled dogs by placing female dogs in heat where wolves could mate with them. So coyote-wolf offspring, which I believe I've seen, share characteristics of both parents. They are nearly as large as a small wolf. They possess the slightly more pointed and fox-like muzzle and ears of the coyote, and some of its nervous attitude as well. These could be accidents of nature. On the other hand, perhaps nature is evolving to fit the demands of a human-changed world.

In the past four or five decades, an animal has appeared in the American northeast that appears to be a coyote but is larger. Could nature be crafting a new canid? Wolves had supposedly been eliminated from the region, though it seems possible that wolves might undertake occasional incursions from Canada. With wolves gone, wouldn't coyotes benefit from becoming larger and more wolf-like, and from being able to feed on the burgeoning white-tailed deer population? And wouldn't wolves, whatever few  might have wandered in or remained hidden in the few remaining large tracts of wilderness, have benefited by becoming more coyote-like—that is, craftier about avoiding humans? Could nature be creating a gene reservoir in the new and larger coyote, a means of saving at least a part of the wolf?

I admit that this is pure speculation. But no matter the reason, these crossbreedings do occur. The common belief that wolves and coyotes don't exist within the same range is false. At Ravenwood, I see both wolves and coyotes almost daily. From my observations on two continents, the relationship between the two predators seems similar to the one that exists between the jackal and the large predators of Africa. Like a pride of lions followed by jackals, I've seen wolves trot down a trail, only to be followed a minute later by a coyote. The coyote, following at a respectful distance, takes advantage of the wolves by scavenging their kills after they leave, a common occurrence near Ravenwood.

Obviously, this is of no advantage to the wolves, for they lose the chance to come back and clean up their kills. But it is of great advantage to the coyote which, while grabbing a snowshoe hare or ruffed grouse along the way, can find an additional bite to eat after the wolves have left.

I have no doubt that the wolf fails to appreciate this arrangement. Wolves must occasionally attack and kill a coyote, for coyotes are extremely wary when they approach a wolf kill. These coyote killings have undoubtedly led to the belief that the two species don't coexist in the same range. Coyotes would probably flourish in the absence of wolves, but they don't vanish simply because wolves are present. They become more cautious. I've watched coyotes approach a carcass with an almost psychotic nervousness, crouching, ears laid back, nearly groveling, suspicious of every movement. Sometimes they sit on a hill and watch a carcass for half an hour or more before attempting to approach it. Often they'll timidly turn and leave without approaching, ill at ease with the situation.

It's difficult to sneak up on a wolf.

Yet I've often heard a pair of coyotes in the forest, barking and yipping at wolves on a kill. It is risky to attach human emotions to an animal, but the coyotes sound angry, perhaps frustrated by the presence of wolves.

Ravens react differently to wolves and coyotes. I commonly see ravens feeding at a carcass along with wolves. The wolves usually ignore the ravens. Coyotes and ravens will also share a site, but while ravens sometimes taunt wolves, they are more respectful of coyotes. Coyotes occasionally lunge and snap at the ravens and, considering that a coyote is faster and more agile than a wolf, the ravens are probably killed just often enough to instill caution.

I have on rare occasion found evidence that something caught and killed a raven while the bird was scavenging. Since I believe the raven is in many ways the smartest creature in the forest, whatever might catch one must also possess a high degree of craftiness—like a coyote, for example. One must also consider that, when ravens and coyotes feed at the same abandoned wolf kill, they are competitors, both filling the ecological niche of scavenger. It is likely that the two species of scavengers might regard each other as rivals.

All that aside, the wolf is the apex predator in much of its range. It certainly is, and has been for ages, the top predator in the forest of Ravenwood. The intelligence of the wolf, combined with its cooperative hunting technique, allows it to best exploit the deer and moose. By killing large animals, wolves need to hunt less often than if they hunted small game—that is, of course, if the large prey are vulnerable and of sufficient numbers.

Think of it in terms of calories per package. How many snowshoe hares would a pack of wolves have to catch in order to equal a white-tailed deer— let alone a moose? How much more energy would they need to expend in

those chases, compared to what's needed when they attack a deer? When seen from this perspective, it becomes clear why wolves hunt the way they do. It is a survival technique evolved over long ages, one that maximizes food intake while minimizing effort.

Two facets of the wolf's hunting technique that I admire are the wolf's nearly unlimited patience during a hunt; and its keen perception of prey animals. Wolves can perceive subtle changes in an animal, even if the individual is one of many in a herd. On Ellesmere Island, I've watched wolves follow musk-oxen relentlessly—not in chase, but in a steady, glaring surveillance. During this preliminary round, the wolves study each animal in the herd.

Similarly, wolves in the northwoods will follow one animal for miles, maybe even for days. They may choose to leave the herd or the single moose or deer untested. But if they detect something amiss, they will test the intended quarry. They might detect a stiffness in an older musk-oxen's gait, or a moose's blindness in one eye—an injury suffered during a sparring match with another rutting bull. Often, the key that marks an animal for attack is not visible to humans. You might even consider this relentless surveillance a test of an animal's spirit, because the wolves are not always watching for a physical defect. Psychological weakness can doom a musk-ox or a moose just as readily. Naïveté is dangerous in the wild, and a young, foolish deer may never become an old, wise deer if wolves are watching. A calf that likes to stray from its protective mother may likewise have a short life. And I believe that some animals simply can't bear for long the penetrating stare of the wolf. Their mental weakness causes them to break and run, when breaking and running is the wrong thing to do.

Some native people believe that the wolves' ability to pick out weak or stupid

WOLVES ON THE TRAIL OF A MOOSE.

fifty-four

creatures is mystical or psychic. The ability may appear psychic even to a dispassionate observer, but it is probably no more than a highly evolved ability to sense through all senses. Wolves see in their prey what you and I cannot—not because they are magical, but because such sensing is one of many things they are better at than we are, although humans do possess a similar skill.

That wolves can sense vulnerability in their prey should not surprise us. Why is it, for instance, that muggers attack certain people but not others? Why is it that people who are afraid of dogs are the ones who most often get bitten? Apparently, neither humans nor dogs have entirely lost the ability to judge, by observing the minute details of body language, the vulnerability of the creature they are about to accost. It is significant that police and security professionals advise vulnerable persons to carry themselves with an air of confidence. Doing so may help them avoid being "preyed upon."

Through the ages, the wolf's persistence has led people to believe that wolves are devious or evil. Imagine a simple herdsman tending his flock. Looking up, he sees wolves sitting at the edge of the forest, studying his sheep. The wolves are patient. They stay for hours. Perhaps they appear again and again over the course of a few days. Finally, they attack and kill a sheep. The period of waiting must seem to the herdsman as awful as the loss of a sheep. A premeditated act—especially an act that causes loss—has always been deemed evil by humans. In this case, though, the wolves' premeditation was comprised of no more malice than the premeditation involved in planning your trip to the supermarket next Saturday.

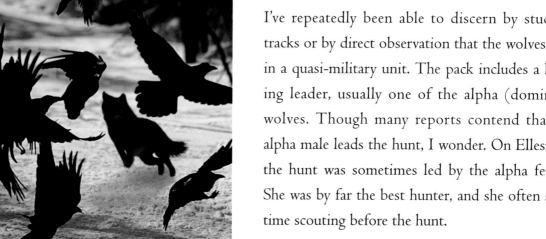

As I looked down upon the skeleton of the moose at that first kill site, I asked some questions that were long in being answered. It wasn't until Ellesmere Island that I began to understand the hows and whens of wolves on a hunt. On several occasions and at close range, I accompanied the Arctic wolf pack as they searched out musk oxen, planned an attack, then sometimes made a kill. My experiences at Ravenwood filled in some of the gaps, even though I've been unable to view a hunt in the dense forest as clearly as I could on the frozen plains of the Arctic. But I have little doubt now that the wolves of Ravenwood use much the same techniques as their white relatives to the north.

I've repeatedly been able to discern by studying tracks or by direct observation that the wolves hunt in a quasi-military unit. The pack includes a hunting leader, usually one of the alpha (dominant) wolves. Though many reports contend that the alpha male leads the hunt, I wonder. On Ellesmere, the hunt was sometimes led by the alpha female. She was by far the best hunter, and she often spent time scouting before the hunt.

Rules are made to be broken, as they say, and that is as true in nature as it is in our own society. There are always exceptions, as in the case of Midback, the alpha female that excelled at hunting. Science is so busy trying to write things down, trying to squeeze things into comfortable niches, trying to measure everything, that it may fail to adequately report just how frequently the exceptions occur.

I've seen a pack try to awaken its sleeping leader. The pack members are

obviously anxious to hunt, but they do not set out until the leader is ready, and the hunt is usually prefaced by a rousing chorus of howls. There is an air of excitement as the wolves get ready, a building of camaraderie, a joyousness. It isn't so very different than the behavior of your own dog when you announce that you're taking her out for a walk or some other excursion: You see a raised level of intensity, a fear of being left behind, happy relief at being underway, and a seriousness about the excursion.

If wolves don't know where their prey is located at the moment, they certainly know where to look. To some it may appear that wolves wander in their hunt. It is a mistake to assume that. They know nearly every tree, every rock, and every creek in their large territories. Because prey animals aren't randomly sprinkled about the woods, but instead concentrate in the habitat that suits them best, wolves move from pocket to pocket, looking for that prey. If one of the wolves has been out scouting prior to the hunt, it may lead the pack directly to the quarry. Even if the distance is great, the wolves move tirelessly, driven to hunt by the need to eat or to feed their pups.

On Ellesmere, I set out on a four-wheeled, all-terrain vehicle to follow a hunting pack. Led by the alpha female, the pack members moved in a nearly straight line, a distance of 30 kilometers from their den, directly to a herd of musk-oxen. Only a few days before, I had observed the alpha female watching this herd. Though I was confused by her behavior at the time, I understood it later when I crested a rise and saw that she had led her pack directly to the oxen in the valley beyond. On her scouting trip, she must have noted that this herd had calves. The wolves eventually killed one of the calves.

Kills aren't pretty. They are mostly an act of teamwork, as a calf is separated from its mother or a lone animal is surrounded and tested. If death is to be,

A PORTRAIT OF WILD BUT CALM INTELLIGENCE.

it comes in spurts, slower than we humans would like, comprised of much bucking by the prey as wolf after wolf lunges in to secure its powerful jaws. If a wolf can grab the head or muzzle, the animal is twisted to the ground. If not, the sheer weight of the wolves, combined with their tugging and the exhaustion of the prey, usually drags the animal to its death. Once on the ground, there is no hope at all for the prey.

Just as the lion does not lie with the lamb, the wolf will not lie with the fawn. Nature is not a theme park, nor a sterile television program in which warm, fuzzy creatures exist in peace and harmony. Wolves hunt in order to kill. And they kill in order to eat.

But their purpose mitigates our human reaction to the death of their prey. I have watched wolves consume their quarry and then, with an immediacy born of purpose, return quickly to their den. Upon returning, the adults are mobbed by hungry pups, their muzzles licked by the mob of young ones. The adults regurgitate a portion of the kill, which is hungrily consumed by the growing puppies. This devoted sharing of food with the young is an admirable quality, and is another example of the wolves' highly social pack behavior. Thus, death becomes life, and "bloodthirsty killers" become a caring family.

I feel about wolves something just short of jealousy. I am in awe. Their persistence, their endurance, and their strength are beyond human capacity—this became painfully apparent as I followed them for days. Perhaps, like the hungry coyotes barking at wolves from the forest, I am forced merely to follow.

BARED TEETH ARE A WARNING.

THE ALPHA PAIR EATS FIRST.

fifty-nine

BROTHER WOLF

T he wind blows sharply across the frigid plain. From a ridge atop a foothill, a dozen prone hunters eye hungrily the small herd of bison grazing below. The hunters talk in quiet, excited whispers.

Their problem is immense, but simple. They are cold, tired, and hungry. Enough food for everyone is grazing within sight. They simply need to get near enough to kill and then eat it.

The hunters study the wind, the way the grass moves, the undulations of the winter-seared prairie. Lying on their stomachs in the tall grass, arms protruding from animal-skin clothing, they draw maps in the dust with their cold-stiffened fingers. A successful hunting plan is desperately needed.

Across the prairie, another group of hunters has discovered the bison. These hunters patiently study the herd. They have spotted youngsters in the herd and know they need only separate one calf from a cow in order to make a kill.

One of the ridgetop hunters sees movement on the prairie. He points silently as four of the rival hunters creep slowly but deliberately through the grass, moving toward the complacent herd, making no attempt to hide, approaching in the wind so the bison can smell the danger. Why, the hunters atop the hill wonder, would the others so foolishly betray their presence?

Frustrated, but fascinated, they observe the rival hunters' technique.

Scenting and then spotting these hunters, the bison pace and snort, tossing curved horns and woolly, massive heads from side to side. A few of the nervous ones stomp repeatedly in place, blowing loudly. A calf bellows. The entire herd turns to watch the approaching threat.

A low hill looms at the bison's backs. The hunters on the ridge watch as two forms material- ize just beyond the crest of the hill, downwind from the bison, moving stealthily through the tall grass to a point behind the rise. Almost nonchalantly, these hunters wait in their hidden position. The hunters on the ridge top smile knowingly.

On the prairie, the four stalking hunters suddenly become charging hunters, running furiously toward the herd. The pan- icked bison wheel, kicking heels and frozen dust into the air, to mix with their chaotic bellows and groans. The hunters close in, darting near, causing some bison to split from the herd, then splintering these animals from one another. The herd begins to thunder off, but one cow and one calf are separated from the rest. The hunters herd these animals to the hilltop, where the two hidden hunters have risen to a ready crouch.

With wild eyes, the cow sees the two waiting hunters materialize in the grey grass. She blows a mighty bellow, calling her calf, and pivots violently to the left, throwing clods of turf. The calf turns, but too late. While one hunter drives the cow away, the other turns the calf from its mother. Five hunters now chase the calf, breathing hard in the lust of pursuit. The final hunter abandons the cow, which stands helplessly only yards away, as if pondering the wis- dom of trying to rescue her calf. Slowly she turns and pounds after the distant herd. In a moment, the kicking, bellowing calf is down, then dead. The hunters circle the prone form,

lifting their voices in a song of excitement and thanks.

Above the frozen prairie, the men on the windswept ridgetop are stunned. Their fists are clenched, and spurts of empathetic adrenaline course through their veins. They gulp air, having almost forgotten to breathe. In amazement they look at one another, forgetting the cold and their hunger for the moment, electrified by the drama they have just witnessed. Its lesson will not be lost on them.

The hunters rise and follow the fleeing bison herd, maintaining a respectful distance from the wolves, which are now consuming the freshly killed calf.

According to Ojibwa mythology, Nanabush, son of mortal woman and the West Wind, learned how to hunt from the wolf. He learned the wolves' meth- ods; he was also taught the taboo against the wanton killing of game.

When Nanabush proved incapable of keeping up with the pack as they pursued caribou, he was left with Tooth, the grandson of the old she-wolf pack leader. The two of them were to hunt moose in the valley, she said, but she warned them to take only the meat they could use. In the intoxication of the hunt, they ignored the she-wolf's warning. As a result, they themselves were hunted by the spirit Manitou, who sought to punish them.

Tooth, the impetuous young wolf, was caught and killed, but Nanabush

YEARLING WOLVES AT PLAY.

MOOSE LAKE: GATEWAY TO THE WILDERNESS.

A WOLF PACK IS A FAMILY. THE AVERAGE LITTER CONSISTS OF SIX PUPS THAT ARE SIGHTLESS AT BIRTH. ALL PACK MEMBERS—BROTHERS, SISTERS, AUNTS, AND UNCLES—COOPERATE IN FEEDING AND WATCHING OVER THE YOUNG. HERE, A RESEARCH PACK CARES FOR ITS PUPS. THE MOTHER IS MOVING THE PUPS BECAUSE RESEARCHERS HAVE DISTURBED THEM. BELOW, THE PACK LISTENS ATTENTIVELY TO THE SQUEAKING OF PUPS DEEP IN THEIR DEN. WOLVES IN THE WILD WILL MOVE PUPS TO KEEP THEM FREE OF DISEASE AND VERMIN THAT ACCUMULATE IN THE DEN.

My canoe glides silently into a secret bay.

bravely stole Tooth's pelt from the spirits. Half-god himself, he brought the wolf back to life. Tooth had already traveled the pathways of the dead, and the resurrected wolf taught Nanabush about those paths, so that he in turn could instruct his people. After Tooth had described the treacherous pathway to heaven, Nanabush sent him back to the land of the dead, where he forever guides our souls as we make the journey to a better world.

And so, according to the legend, the wolf is our brother, our teacher in the hunt, our partner in crimes, and our guide to heaven.

The Ojibwa were the last of the native people to inhabit Ravenwood country, and their story reveals what I have long suspected: that man may have learned much about survival from Brother Wolf.

From the beginning, humans and wolves were much alike. Both are apex predators. Both human tribes and wolf packs consist largely of familial units. Both rely on a strong social structure to govern society and the hunt (which in turn ensures survival of the society). Both elect, in their own ways, leaders possessing great craft or physical prowess. And in both societies, elaborate rituals reinforce relationships, maintain order, and enforce discipline.

The Ojibwa legend offers a non-European view of the wolf that stands in stark and majestic contrast to the senseless wolf hatred of Western culture. The Ojibwa and other native groups demonstrate that humans and wolves

can live in close proximity; and that people who are not determined to "conquer" the natural world understand clearly the kinship between humans and Brother Wolf. I have not found a single fearful reference to the wolf in North American aboriginal mythology.

To me, there is little doubt that the fictional scene at the beginning of this chapter is based on more than just speculation; that, like most myths, it is based on a germ of reality.

I have lived with and observed some of the few remaining "primitive" human societies. I use the term in quotations because these cultures are or were extremely rich, their science elaborate, and their relationship to nature direct and responsible. Only from a materialistic and technological perspective can the term "primitive" be applied, and even then the label is arrogant and inaccurate. They have technologies. Their technologies are simply different than ours.

A common characteristic possessed by humans who still survive as hunter-gatherers is their intimate familiarity with the world around them. They are careful observers. They watch, and they learn. To believe that our ancient ancestors, who knew the wolf well, did not watch and learn from it would be foolish. No hunter, ancient or modern, can watch wolves execute a hunt without being filled with great admiration. And if ancient people were impressed with the wolf's strategy, they would naturally try to duplicate the plan and the results. Bear in mind that these peoples' hunting success was measured by survival, not in pleasant memories of days afield. No kill, no dinner—and perhaps no

A WOLF IS SURPRISED WHILE HUNTING BEAVER.

PICTOGRAPHS THROUGHOUT NORTH AMERICA TELL US THE WOLF WAS REVERED BY EARLY NATIVE AMERICAN PEOPLES. BELOW, NEAR THE BOUNDARY WATERS, A PICTOGRAPH FROM HEGMAN LAKE DEPICTS A WOLF CHASING A MOOSE, WITH THE ALL-POWERFUL SPIRIT KNOWN AS *MAY-MAY-GWAY-SHI* PRESIDING. AT RIGHT, A VERTICAL CLIFF AT LAC LA CROIX ALSO FEATURES THE POWERFUL FIGURE OF THE WOLF. THE SPIRITUAL SIGNIFICANCE THAT THE WOLF HELD FOR ANCIENT CULTURES IS AS MYSTERIOUS AS THE AURORA BOREALIS THAT ILLUMINATES THE RAVENWOOD SKY.

clothing. Under these circumstances, the notion that early people emulated other predators becomes a highly believable hypothesis.

I have watched excited wolves gather to hunt, and watched as they circled and surrounded a herd of musk-oxen using a technique like the one outlined in the opening of this chapter. How miraculous this technique would seem if you were the one to whom it was revealed! It would be an exciting new survival technology, based on ambush rather than chase. Too simple to be marvelous? Consider the simplicity of the wheel.

I believe that humans learned stealth and ambush techniques from wolves. However, I'm not confident that the learning was mutual. As far as I can tell, the only thing wolves have learned from humans is to keep their distance.

Though in recent times humans have hated or feared wolves (with the notable exception of some native peoples), I doubt that wolves and humans hated each other in ancient times as Hollywood and some popular writers would like us to believe. Unless predators are competing for a finite or dwindling resource, they tend to maintain a casual but respectful distance from each other. Humans were more likely to tolerate a pack of hunting wolves than to tolerate another tribe of hunting humans. Wolves display the same territorial tendencies: They can tolerate hunters of other species, but they will attempt to drive out competing wolves.

In early times we possessed no domesticated animals. Wolves, then, were

not a threat to our cattle or sheep, for these animals were wild. They belonged as much to the wolves as to us. Without ownership, there is no possessiveness and little resentment. In a world of plenty, there is little incentive for rivalry.

At what point, I wonder, did early people first notice the qualities we share with wolves? In many ways, we are more similar to wolves than we are to other primates. The great apes are dependent on forests; humans and wolves survive on open plains, tundra, mountains, and broken forests. Apes are largely vegetarian. Wolves and humans evolved as carnivores—and as hunters that operate in cooperative units. Both wolves and early humans were about the same body weight. Both preyed upon the same species, many of which were large. Both humans and wolves are more intelligent than their prey; only through strategy and brief but intense exertion can wolves and humans kill prey that possess greater speed or strength.

Humans and wolves spend proportionally about the same percentage of their lifetimes as sexually immature juveniles, a period of learning and training. Cooperation among our "packs" centers around survival of the young. Leadership is paramount to the success of each society, and those who challenge it are reprimanded for the benefit of the larger community.

Being a carnivore carries specific traits—traits we do not share with our vegetarian primate relatives. For instance, because carnivores eat higher on the food chain, they must draw from a larger territory and live in small family

In a rare wilderness moment, a wolf allowed me to lie down within 30 feet.

No prey is too small: a wolf pounces on a deer mouse.

units. A carnivore subsists on other animals that turn vegetable matter into meat, and meat has more food value by volume than vegetables. Whereas grazing animals spend most of their time feeding, carnivores spend most of their time socializing, resting, and traveling, a workable lifestyle because their food comes in concentrated form. Though hunting is critical to the carnivore's survival, it is not the most time-consuming behavior, especially among those that prey upon large animals. Kills need occur only infrequently. But because the large prey animals have longer gestation periods and lower reproductive rates, predator-prey balance must be maintained in order to ensure the survival of both species. Both humans and wolves occupy this ecological niche.

The hominid ancestors of our race apparently evolved on the plains of Africa as highly mobile predators of medium-sized animals. They were widespread and successful—so successful that, after expanding throughout the continent, they moved on to colonize the rest of the world. Africa also happens to be one of the very few places to which wolves have never spread—perhaps they found their niche already occupied. Other than humans, wolves are the most widespread animal in the northern hemisphere.

Territoriality is an important aspect of both human and wolf society, because of the need to "control" the harvest of game. But there are other advantages to claiming a territory. Good territory provides a predictable supply of food. When you occupy a territory for a long time, you learn every detail of the landscape; you know the movements of other animals and the best places to lie in ambush. Knowing your territory allows you to find your way around in the dark or in poor weather. When you've seen the behavior of other animals during particular seasons or weather, you know where to look for them. In other words, you can more efficiently extract food from your territory.

A GREAT GRAY OWL SEARCHES FOR RODENTS.

THE ALPHA PAIR

seventy-four

For the wolf, good den sites are important and sometimes hard to find. Being able to control one, to place it in a safe spot within a territory, is a boon to survival. Similarly, early humans must have cherished a good home base, an area offering shelter, water, and ease of defense.

Nature is not always stable. The more control you can exert over the number of prey animals killed, where and how you raise your young, and the odds of finding food when needed, the more stability your tribe or pack can achieve. Possessing a territory adds stability, and it is likely that the search for stability led us to the domestication of both plants and animals, thus ensuring a reliable food supply in the face of a growing human population.

Population control—limits on tribe or pack density within a territory—is critical to both human hunter-gatherers and wolf packs. There is strong evidence indicating that wolves respond to fluctuations in the prey base by slowing or increasing their own reproductive rate. In any case, only the alpha pair generally breeds, while the entire pack works to feed, protect, and raise the pups. In addition to controlling their breeding, wolves disperse from existing packs in order to establish new territories. Sometimes new wolves join an existing pack decimated by disease or accident. This not only helps bolster pack size, but introduces new genetic material.

I believe that the exchange of animals between packs happens more often than is commonly thought. While there is strong, documented evidence that wolves vigorously defend their territory against marauding packs, fighting

even to the death, we also know that many wolves choose to leave their pack for parts unknown. Since there is a finite amount of space to which they can flee—much of it already occupied by other wolves—finding an unoccupied territory cannot be easy. Some lone wolves are killed when they are caught in territory belonging to other packs, but it seems unlikely that all are dispatched in this manner. It is also unlikely that they readily find unoccupied country in which to start anew. My experiences at Ellesmere, confirmed by my observations at Ravenwood, indicate to me that pack membership changes from year to year, and that new wolves make inroads into established packs. For whatever reasons—size, strength, cunning, or subservience—outside wolves are integrated into established packs, and this integration must prove beneficial to the survival of all or it would not occur.

Beyond all this, it seems to me that wolves genuinely enjoy traveling through the countryside. Humans relish travel as well, and we have certainly dispersed from our tribes in order to start new colonies. We have always been explorers, and part of that urge is the need to establish new territories of our own.

The size of wolves' territories increases as one goes farther north, a phenomenon that was probably true for early human hunters as well. The reason is simple: Prey density is lower in the far north than in warmer climes. The wolves I observed on Ellesmere occupied an enormous territory. Because snow allowed me to track my study pack, and because I was able to use an all-terrain vehicle to follow the wolves and accurately measure the distances traveled, I was able to establish the size of the area they ranged. Normally

this is a difficult thing to do, requiring the use of a radio collar. On the barrens of the Arctic, I found that it was entirely possible for the pack's territory to include up to 4,000 square miles. I state this here because some scientists, who have spent little time actually following wolves, disputed the claim when I first made it in *White Wolf*—this despite the fact that I measured it personally, mile by mile. Robert Ream, a professor at the University of Montana, claimed in *Natural History* magazine that my figures were not valid because an ocean fjord was located only a few miles from the den site. The fjord, he stated, would effectively block the wolves' movement in that direction, thus making my measurements erroneous. Ream, however, observed this pack of six only during the brief, ice-free summer. Had he devoted any length of time to his study, he might have realized that the fjord is locked in ice during the majority of the year, opening its far shore and the country beyond to these wolves. Because I virtually lived with the wolves, I was well aware of the territorial enlargement caused by the freeze-over. Seasonal changes in territorial size are common among wolves, especially among those that feed on highly mobile, herd-grazing animals.

By adjusting their reproductive rates (alpha females usually ensure that subordinates do not breed), wolves generally maintain a population well below the full capacity of the pack's territory. Human hunter/gatherers, even to this day, also remain in ecological balance. Because the women nurse children for about three years, which seems to affect ovulation (and among some tribes there are taboos about mating with a lactating woman), birth rates are kept low. In other words, both wolves and early humans ensured their survival by regulating their numbers, so that the food source would not be depleted. The technique did not stem from any ecological consciousness. It was simply a sort of savings account. When more food animals existed than were needed, the clan or pack could survive periods of unusual weather, disease within the

prey stock, or disruption of migration patterns. In hard times they could dip into the principal, rather than living on the interest.

That humans are as territorial as wolves almost goes without saying. Witness our ongoing (and unusually brutal) wars over the imaginary lines that separate countries and ethnic "tribes." We also get possessive about property—particularly about real estate. Since I've come to "own" Ravenwood, I see the land in a much different light, one that requires me to nurture and to defend.

My reasons for possessing my territory are not so different than those of the wolves. Though I do not need the animal "food" that grows on my land, I do extract my living from the animals and the land; therefore, I feel the need to exert some control over what happens at Ravenwood. In fact, my wildlife photography requires that control. While some great photographs happen by chance, most happen as a result of planning. Conversely, images that might have been great fail for the lack of suitable background, lighting, or readiness. By ensuring that other humans will not interfere, and by allowing me to become intimately acquainted with the land and its animals, Ravenwood increases my odds of success. It also assures me of a pristine background against which I can compose my work. Earlier inhabitants took food from this land. I make photographs that, when sold, help me buy food extracted from someone else's "territory." I have exchanged a weapon for a camera.

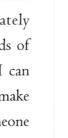

In their territorial struggles, wolves seem to have a more highly developed sense of fairness than humans. They avoid violence whenever possible. Through the use of signals, wolf packs delineate their territory and advertise its boundaries to their neighbors, decreasing the odds of a war-like encounter. Rarely does a pack benefit from territorial transgressions, so the species' survival is enhanced by avoiding such trouble. Wolves also scent-mark their range, much the way a dog marks its neighborhood. By urinating and defecating, wolves leave a message, and these scent-markings become more frequent near territorial borders—which indicates that wolves consider the establishment of boundaries a very important matter.

But there is another means of defining boundaries. I cannot think of any animal that defends its territory more eloquently than does the wolf through its howl. The howl is an auditory fence. It says "we are here" to other wolves, and serves as a long-range warning. Hearing this warning, a foreign wolf has ample time in which to change its course. It may instead choose to enter the territory stealthily, trying to escape detection. In either case, the likelihood of confrontation is minimized, decreasing the chances of death or injury.

Both, however, do occur. About the only time wolves will attack one another is in a territorial dispute, and death often results. Ravenwood neighbor Bob Cary, a wise and talented observer of nature, told me of two wolf packs that met on the frozen surface of a small lake near my cabin a few years ago. The evidence in the snow indicated an intense battle, during which some wolves were killed and their remains eaten by the victors.

Wolves compete for a shred of deer hide.

It is unclear how frequently such encounters occur.

I do know from personal experience just how respectful wolves can be of each other's boundaries. Some years ago, I was dropped by plane into the wilderness, in order to film wolves for the U.S. Forest Service. I had the misfortune of setting up camp at the junction of three pack territories. A noted Minnesota wolf researcher had discovered this boundary area through the use of radio collars, and had suggested the common border as a good spot to attempt filming.

It was a bad suggestion. Though the wolves often responded to my howls, it was all but impossible to view them. My camp was in a "no wolves" zone, like the demilitarized zone in Korea. No wolves would venture in—or even near—this unseen line. They smelled it, heard it, and respected it.

I have had to put up with human interlopers on my land, and as a result I have a certain amount of respect for the fairness of wolves. My interlopers sneak onto my property to fish and camp. If they had asked, I would have given them permission. Instead of asking, they chose all kinds of devious measures, often defacing my property and destroying my signs. I suppose these people feel that asking permission is a subservient act. Perhaps it is, though I don't see it that way. But asking permission serves the same purpose as the wolf's display of subservience: It avoids confrontation. My own primal side is aroused when I catch and confront a trespasser, and it is always a struggle to remain "civilized." Wolves play fair. They give warning of their boundaries and respect those boundaries; I doubt that any transgressions are made except in cases of dire need. No wolf would risk death unless impending death drove it to do so—as in a starvation winter, which is when most wolf trespassing occurs.

My human trespassers, I sometimes think, just do it out of ornery disrespect for territory.

I have watched an alpha male sit erect, his yellow eyes closed peacefully as a troop of mobbing pups leaped toward his muzzle, each pup paying respect, the father aglow with what I can only describe as great pleasure.

I have seen a teenage wolf tease his younger siblings, roughing them up until they squeal, then watched as the pups continued to dote on him, just as you doted on your big brother or sister even though he or she sometimes tormented you.

From my cabin window, I've seen excited young wolves, grown sexually mature, trying to mate with their gray wolf mother, only to be viciously attacked by her. Mating with one's mother is not acceptable in human or wolf society.

I've listened and observed as wolves prepared for the hunt, singing and virtually dancing in their excitement. I've watched hunter-gatherer peoples behave in much the same way.

I've followed wolves as they carried home a part of their kill in order to share food with the young ones or with other pack members who were unable to attend the hunt.

And I've seen wolves greet each other, the submissive ones lowering themselves before the dominant pack member, licking the alpha's face, tucking their tails between their legs. I've also watched humans "lower themselves" in the face of power or the perception of power.

There are so many similarities between the two species that it is small wonder that the wolf fascinates us. Though humans and wolves are unrelated genetically, the wolf provides a remarkable study of how our early hunter-gatherer societies might have lived and evolved. We hunt, eat, socialize, organize, and practice rituals in much the same manner. We fit the same ecosystems and we once maintained a similar ecological balance. We are both territorial.

In all of these behaviors, the Ojibwa hunters of Ravenwood country saw something familiar and admirable, as did Native Americans elsewhere. They saw in the wolf a high degree of skill, intelligence, endurance, and strength. Their respect is visible in the aging, blood-colored pictographs painted on rock cliffs throughout North America. They saw a teacher. They saw a brother. They saw themselves.

Somehow as the ages passed, Western people began attributing aspects of evil to the wolf: maliciousness, thievery, murderousness.

What they saw wasn't the wolf. But they, too, were seeing themselves.

WOLVES ARE CAPABLE OF GREAT TENDERNESS.

AN ANCIENT PROMISE

now on the dark forest limbs has turned pink in the cold sunrise. From the north drifts a meager, chill wind. The hunter on the forested ridge tightens his fur collar against it. Shifting silently in caribou

mukluks, he moves cautiously to the edge of the small cliff—as much to bask in the wan warmth of the sun as to peer down into the ancient notch that cuts through the granite ridge. He holds his small bow and two arrows in his mittened left hand and thrusts his bare, ready-to-shoot right hand deep into the folds of his warm clothing.

The caribou are coming. He knows this because only yesterday he heard the ravens tell the wolves with croaking cries. He believed the ravens were wise, and that they conversed with wolves to tell them of pending prey. The scavenging birds know that if the wolves eat well, so will they.

Last night, as he sat with his family in the glow of the smoking lodge fire, the wolves rumored of the caribou as they howled messages to his dogs in the cold darkness. As he watched his dogs, he was assured of the coming caribou by their howled answers and nervous excitement, by the way they sniffed the north wind. He saw the hunger in his dogs' green eyes as they paced wolfishly in the shadows around the camp. He saw, too, the hunger in his family's eyes. Everything awaited the coming of the caribou.

WOLF TALK: I OFTEN HEAR ECHOING HOWLS AT THIS SITE.

In the dark hours of waiting, he offers silent prayers to the Great Spirit, prayers for the spirit of the caribou he would kill, prayers asking for the skill of the wolf in the hunt. And he envisioned the sustenance that the hunt would provide. Quietly he examined his bow, tested the flint tips of his arrows, smoothed the goose-feather fletching with his fingers.

Now, as the hunt was about to begin, he thought again of those prayers and preparations. Earlier, the snow muffled his approach in the darkness through the aspens and pines to the watching point above the notch in the ridge. Each year, after the freezing of the lakes, the caribou moved south to an area of dense pines, where they would eat from branches trailing mosses and find protection from deep snows. Each year, their short migration took them through the narrow gap in the rock ridge. All along their route, hunters waited for or pursued them: wolf, dog, and human.

It was a pact, a covenant among all living things. It was balanced, it was necessary, and it was just. The caribou died so the hunters could live, and the hunters killed only as many as they needed. In turn, the hunters culled the caribou herd, ensuring that it would not grow too large for its supply of forage.

The notch was a good place to wait for the caribou. His father's father had discovered it, and each year they made camp nearby, along the singing brook, to await the gift of the caribou. He had left the warmth of his camp near the murmuring waterfall to stalk out under the white, blazing stars; his brother had also departed, taking the anxious dogs, moving north to the frozen lake. There his brother would hide, and as the caribou crossed the white plain of ice to disappear into the forest, the man and the dogs would move quickly behind them, driving them to the notch in the cliff and the waiting bowman.

He thinks now of his brother, and an excitement stirs in him. He must not fail. The winter will be long, and later the hunting will become more difficult. A cache of caribou meat will keep for months in the frigid weather. He sheds his quiver of arrows and props it within easy reach. Today he will shoot as many caribou as the Great Spirit allows while the caribou pass quickly below. Those that do not die quickly from the sharp slice of his stone-tipped arrows will be hunted down later with the aid of the dogs.

At a distant sound, he stops moving, stops thinking. He bends his head to the north. He closes his eyes to better focus his ears and his mind, and to locate the source of the sound. He tilts his head forward so the ruff on his collar does not rustle in his ears. His wife had plaited his black hair in preparation for the hunt, so that not even this would obstruct his hearing. He holds his breath.

There! The sound is louder now, and it is the sound of hooves shuffling in snow. To the north. Yes. Near the entrance to the notch. His nose flares, muscles tense, knees bend in a ready crouch. He hears the pant of a dog or wolf on the run. Perhaps it is his prize female, in which the wolf ancestor runs so true. A wry smile crosses his lips. She always seems to know where he is, rarely failing to drive the prey to him.

He opens his eyes. Above the valley, he sees a raven waiting silently on a tall snag. Below the notch, he sees movement through the snow-laden branches, then hears the strange, clicking sound of caribou ankles.

Snow flies from spruce boughs as a bull caribou bursts, antlers-first, into the notch. Steam bellows from its muzzle. Now more caribou follow. The dogs are worrying the herd, keeping it moving and together, herding it through the narrow notch. The hunter beseeches the Great Spirit once more, bends his thought to the caribou, bends his bow. The caribou have come.

Timber wolves range from black to nearly white.

PLAY IS A CRITICAL ELEMENT IN THE
DEVELOPMENT OF ALL HIGHER MAMMALS.
FOR WOLVES, PLAY IS NOT ONLY ESSENTIAL TO
THE DEVELOPMENT OF INDIVIDUALS, BUT ALSO
TO ESTABLISHING AND MAINTAINING PACK
HIERARCHY. WOLVES CHALLENGE AND TEST
THEIR PREY; ON A LESS DEADLY LEVEL, PLAY
IS ONE WAY IN WHICH THEY CHALLENGE
AND TEST EACH OTHER. THEIR GAMES OFTEN
RESEMBLE TAG OR HIDE AND SEEK.

When the glaciers retreated northward from Ravenwood country, a rocky tundra grew in their wake. Hunters followed the game animals, which followed the plants, which followed the retreating glacier. One of those hunters was the wolf. Another was man. A third was probably the dog.

Across the northern tier of America, that exodus of ice occurred 10,000 to 12,000 years ago. Paleo-Indians were part of the scene then, and with them traveled what I believe was a most significant technology. That technology had been discovered elsewhere as well—in the Middle East, Europe, and Asia. Independent of one another, groups of human hunters across the globe had either stumbled upon or brilliantly mastered our first partnership with a wild animal.

That animal was the wolf. The relationship was mutually beneficial. And after a long association with humans, *Canis lupus*, the wolf, became *Canis familiaris*, the dog.

Today's genetic tests can discriminate between the DNA of a wolf and that of a coyote, a jackal, or a fox. But the tests cannot discern a difference between a wolf and a dog. So far, science has been unable to find a genetic marker that distinguishes a dog's DNA from a wolf's, though the two can be separated by studying enzymes or skulls. Simply put, the wolf is *the* dog—the dog from which all domesticated breeds have sprung. When you see the gray wolf, you see the archetypal dog, the prototype, the progenitor.

Archaeological evidence proves that humans and dogs lived together at least

12,000 years ago. By this time, purposeful or accidental changes in the wolf/dog's breeding had created a few physical traits that separated the dog from the wolf. When the wolf became the dog, it lost its longer muzzle, resulting in the development of a forehead and the crowding of teeth on the foreshortened jawbone. The shorter jaw resulted in dental overlap as the teeth were packed together. These two features comprise the archaeological means of distinguishing between the two species.

The changes must have occurred slowly. For thousands of years, the animal was perhaps neither clearly wolf nor dog. Only in very recent times have the dog breeds we are familiar with been developed through selective breeding. It may seem difficult to believe that a Pekinese is the descendant of a wolf. Yet the differences between the two can be explained by virtue of human intervention in breeding.

Most working dogs, from shepherds to retrievers, retain the essential build and bones of the wolf. And the genes of any species—dogs, humans, and others—allow for a wide range of physical features. Humans, for example, display a wide range of hair, skin, and eye coloring, as do dogs. Humans range in size from the most diminutive races to the tallest—not unlike the size range found among dogs. Scientists once believed that, after the wolf became the dog, it bred with related, dog-like species such as the jackal, further influencing the wide variety of shapes and sizes found in *Canis familiaris*. More recently, though, the accepted theory is that only the wolf contributed to the genes of the dog.

A WOLF ON THE MOVE AT -30 DEGREES.

The family Canidae is comprised of all wild and domesticated dogs. It includes our pets as well as wolves, foxes, coyotes, and jackals—some 35 living species worldwide. Members of this family are native to all continents except Antarctica and Australia. The Australian dingo, now a wild dog, is thought to be a form of domestic dog brought to that continent by aboriginal humans, an animal that has since reverted to a wild existence.

Some nine million years ago, the ancestors of today's canids began to take forms that we would recognize as types of wolves, jackals, and foxes, apparently evolving in what is now North America. About eight million years ago, during the Miocene era, these animals migrated to Asia, eventually spreading to the European continent.

It is thought that about two million years ago, some of these animals, which had continued to evolve in Asia, returned to the North American continent during the many migrations of that period. During this time, for instance, the dire wolf, a form of wolf that became extinct in relatively recent times, persisted in North America.

Exactly when humans and wolves formed their primal pact is unknown, but we do know that dog remains have been discovered in human habitations as old as 12,000 years. In the Natufian region of northern Israel, a dog-puppy skeleton was found with the remains of a human. The two were obviously buried together.

Domesticated dog remains have also been unearthed at sites in England

(about 11,000 years old) and in Idaho (at least 10,000 years old). These dates all precede the invention of farming and the domestication of any other animal. In some cases, earlier sites have been discovered where the remains cannot be clearly defined as either wolf or dog, and where it is unclear whether the animals lived with humans.

The Israeli site is the most telling. It clearly shows that some type of relationship existed between humans and dogs, because the two were buried together. The left hand of the human was found across the puppy's chest, as if cradling it.

Archaeology continues to push back the dates of all of our race's endeavors and achievements. Considering that early people who had somehow become affiliated with the wolf had little reason to change the animal, and that the wolf/dog is our very first venture into domestication, I feel safe in speculating that evidence will someday indicate a relationship between the two species dating back as far as 20,000 or even 30,000 years, and that the change from wolf to dog took a very long time. After all, our original purpose in allying ourselves with the wolf was most likely for hunting—a function for which the wolf was already well-adapted. A partnership would require little change except in temperament. Wolves do not make good pets, but these early people weren't looking for lap dogs.

Today we find some of the wolf's traits undesirable in a companion. Wolves are "high-strung." They are prone to chewing and other destructive acts. They are not "house-broken," nor can they be trained in this way, and

Wolves roll in otter scat.

they're perhaps too aggressive. However, these traits would have been much more tolerable among a tribe of hunter-gatherers. Wolves could have fit into early human societies with little adaptation.

Very early sites, yet to be discovered, may well reveal true wolf skeletons in association with humans. The difficulty then will lie in deciding whether we merely killed and ate the wolf, or whether humans and the wolf killed together and ate together. It would not have been necessary to cohabit with wolves in order to establish a relationship with them. Full-time partnering and eventual domestication may have occurred long after the two species became acquainted and began working together. This symbiotic relationship between wolves and humans may have rewarded both species with the distinction of becoming the two most widespread mammals on earth.

Wolves sometimes follow people around, a trait that makes my neighbors near Ravenwood quite nervous. Some attribute this to simple curiosity, while others fear for their lives. No doubt the former is more accurate—not just because a wolf is an intelligent animal likely to be curious, but because for aeons the wolf has associated humans with food. Here in Minnesota, wolves often eat wounded deer that have escaped human hunters—and these are hunters whose sophisticated weapons make the loss of a deer much less likely than it was for our Stone Age ancestors.

To think that wolves were not aware of our ancestors' hunting activities— the same wolves that know every hill, every tree, and every brook in their

territory—is foolish. Early humans must have had a high incidence of failure when hunting, despite their superior skills, because of their primitive weaponry. Since wolves often rely upon finding prey that has a defect or vulnerability, the practice of following human hunters would have been a profitable venture. In this manner wolves could capture wounded prey that had escaped. In addition, although aboriginal hunters made (and make) excellent use of most parts of a kill, there are scraps wolves relish that we do not. Trailing behind us would let the wolves find and consume these morsels. We might have become an environmental factor in the wolf's feeding—making hunting easier and much more predictable for the wolf than looking for prey weakened by age or disease. Following humans is probably a behavior that dates back to the wolf's earliest encounters with people.

Such early associations not only seem reasonable, but I believe they were common. And it is likely that we in turn profited at the wolf's expense. Though no human hunter could keep up with a pack of hunting wolves, we must occasionally have stumbled upon a recent wolf kill and used fire or weapons to drive the wolves away, thereby claiming the feast. Wolves occasionally kill more than their immediate needs dictate, often caching it for later use. Adept and alert humans must certainly have taken advantage of such easy pickings. I have watched wolves bury parts of carcasses that must have weighed 10 or 15 pounds—a good meal for a small family of humans. It is unlikely that I am the first human who ever noticed this.

There are a few ways to explain how we might have become that first profound case of two species actually living together. All explanations depend on the supposition that wolves and humans were living in near proximity, and that we knew of and tolerated each other. Certainly the animosity that exists in modern times did not then exist; if it had, we would have attempted to kill every wolf we encountered, rather than adopting it as our own.

The beginning of our long relationship could have developed simply. If wolves followed us and fed from our kill, scavenging the scraps, they might simply have become dependent upon us. At Ravenwood, I have seen young, inexperienced wolves become "spoiled" when I have offered them road-killed deer too often. Their ready dependence is easy to understand—scavenging is simpler and far less dangerous than undertaking a kill.

On the other hand, humans might have become dependent upon wolves. We have always looked for the path of least resistance. Driving wolves from a kill, making use of scraps left on a carcass, or collecting wounded prey may well have enhanced our own survival.

Wolves howl excitedly before a hunt. Just as I have been able to locate prey species by watching the wolf den and noting the direction the wolves traveled to or from a hunt, early people may have been alerted by wolves to the presence of game. Certainly no person whose very existence depended upon knowing where game could be found—especially those people who subsisted on herd animals that wandered or migrated—would fail to become more

alert if they learned that wolves were embarking upon a hunt. Even if you could not keep up with the wolves during the actual hunt, be present when the pack made its kill, or be able to make a kill yourself, you need only arrive in time to carve off a chunk of the animal in order to make your effort worthwhile.

This is confirmed by Alaskan wildlife biologist Dr. Victor Van Ballenberghe. As a poor graduate student hungrily tracking and studying wolves by snowshoe in Minnesota, he occasionally excised venison steaks from fresh wolf kills, and believes a hardy soul could subsist through winter by specializing in such scavenging. Early wolf researcher and writer Sigurd Olson relates a similar experience in his essay, "A Mountain Listens," in which he liberates a haunch of venison after witnessing a wolf kill a whitetail doe. The wolf merely retreated while Olson took a share. It is doubtful that these two men were the first to partake of such bounty.

These sorts of scenes must have occurred repeatedly for thousands of years around the globe, as we two similar hunters co-existed by feeding on the same prey. Long before archaeological evidence indicates the presence of the dog, it's certain that we knew Brother Wolf.

Still, at some point we chose to *live* with a wolf—or the wolf chose to live with us. This profound choice could have been the product of happenstance, perhaps when particularly tolerant wolves (each wolf has its distinctive personality) that had become lazy or dependent upon our kills began hanging

WOLVES SEEM TO TRULY ENJOY THE HOWL.

around our camps. Though a wild wolf is not a dog, one thing the two animals share is their devotion to food. If an early human hunter saw the advantage of having wolves around and tossed chunks of meat or bones to them, the wolves would soon associate people with food.

Let me restate here that I doubt whether these people feared wolves. Around the world, predators rarely attack each other, and we truly were a formidable predator. Attacking another predator, one that is not directly threatening you or your livelihood, carries with it only the danger of death or injury. Under such circumstances, developing a partnership with wolves would carry little risk when weighed against the possible advantages.

Perhaps an early Leonardo, a person of great vision, clearly perceived the advantages of partnership with a wolf, and made a conscious choice to relate to this animal. Such an "invention" would rank among the most significant technological advances of our race. Or perhaps a child found a lost pup, brought it home, and raised it. The grown wolf may quickly have demonstrated its value to its adoptive "pack." Perhaps there were many Leonardos or many pup adoptions. But whether the affiliation was an invention or an accident, it has shaped the course of our history to a degree that I believe is both profoundly important and inexplicably overlooked.

While many scientists speculate that we adopted the wolf as an aid to hunting, few have understood the significance of that aid, or the many attendant benefits of having a wolf in the house. Perhaps it is necessary to

spend considerable time in difficult, wild places to understand just how tenuous life can be. In the country around Ravenwood, winter temperatures often plummet to 30 degrees below zero. Wolves, like early humans, must travel widely to find prey, and they must test each animal they see. The deer are wary and swift, and I have read tracks in the snow indicating that a deer has scented wolves near a frozen lakeshore and abruptly changed direction, leaping in a flurry of 12-foot bounds.

Neither a wolf nor a human hunter has an easy time killing such alert and agile prey. The combination of our specialties—the chase and the sharp weapon—undoubtedly provided a new dimension, one that benefited wolf and man. But the wolf and the dog have done more for us than providing able assistance. They have made it possible for us to flourish, and both species have benefited.

Consider the wolf who became the dog. In the United States, outside of Alaska, there are less than 2,000 wolves—most of which roam the Minnesota wilds. Yet in this same territory there are 52 million dogs! Seen strictly as a strategy for the survival of a species, the wolf certainly secured a place in the world for its progeny by becoming the dog.

But people have benefited the most. Imagine the primitive hunter. He is not particularly fast. His weapons are simple, probably limited to spears when he first becomes affiliated with wolves. He is prone to attack and injury when he attempts to kill larger prey. He frequently loses animals that are only wounded.

LOOKING NORTH, THE CANADIAN WILDERNESS LIES ON THE HORIZON.

one hundred one

Enter the wolf/dog. It is fast and has great endurance. It needs no weapons, because it *is* a weapon. It is agile enough to avoid most attacks. It is highly protective, so it could rescue humans from attack—or at the very least, divert the prey's attention while the human escapes or kills the prey animal. And few animals, wounded or otherwise, can elude the senses of the wolf. I have traveled with the Inuit, who used their wolf-like sled dogs to distract polar bears while they dispatched the bears at close range.

Our wolf/dog partner became our first "smart" weapon. Our wolf could run down animals that were too fast for us, grab them, and hold them until our lunging spears finished the kill. It could herd animals to us as we waited in ambush. Swift kills would no longer be necessary, for with a pack of wolves or dogs, wounded animals could scarcely escape. Those same tracking skills could also initiate the hunt and lead us to prey. The dog's senses of smell and hearing are vastly superior to ours, and our success is tremendously enhanced when we hunt together.

All of which is immensely significant.

Better hunting means finding more food while expending less energy. Hunting with the wolf/dog also made acquiring food somewhat less dangerous. With more food, more energy, and less danger, we are likely to be healthier and live longer. Being better providers, we create more and healthier offspring. We have the time to develop tools, ornaments, and clothing from the animals we eat. With the wolf/dog, we are also much more mobile, for we can use them as pack animals to transport our food back to camp.

Think of that advantage. With pack animals, a whole new lifestyle could evolve. We could maintain a more permanent home, because hunters could venture farther afield and still carry significant burdens home. I once owned a large malamute named Chinook. Frequently this animal carried loads of camera gear for me into remote areas, loads that certainly approached 30 pounds. Imagine how efficiently you could transport large quantities of food if you had the help of six such animals.

Our own migrations could have expanded greatly through the use of pack dogs. Spanish explorers who penetrated the American plains before Indians used horses found tribes moving entire villages by using pack trains of 500 dogs. I doubt that such use was a recent development.

Guardianship has long been a role played by our dogs. Undoubtedly those who preceded us discovered early this valuable attribute in their canine companions. While they were hunting away from home, their extra wolves or dogs could guard the family back at the camp. Being by nature a territorial pack animal, the wolf could easily transfer its allegiance to a human "pack," a trait we encourage even today. Think of the significance of having such protectors! Old and young could be left in camp while the hunters and gatherers went afield, confident that their loved ones were guarded by loyal sentinels.

I remember getting a full night's sleep while camping along a pass through

Taking charge: an early indication of dominance.

the Canadian Rockies that was regularly being used by a grizzly bear. I slept confidently because my malamute, Chinook, was performing double-duty as an early-warning alarm system. Anyone who has slept in bear country knows the comfort of sharing the tent with a protective dog. The significance of a good night's sleep should not be underestimated. A family in its cave or lodge could rest securely, knowing that marauding predators would be driven away by the wolf/dogs, or that the dogs would at least alert them to the attack.

With more peace of mind, more mobility, more food, and better health, people must have had more "leisure" time in which to think and create. Humans began to flourish some 20,000 to 30,000 years ago, inventing new and better tools and weapons, and developing elaborate cultures and beliefs that are evident at burial sites and in cave art. How much of this advancement can we attribute to our cooperation with the wolf/dog? Is the rapid expansion of our race around the globe during this period also related? Did those things that leave little archaeological evidence, perishable or abstract items such as clothing, language, and intellect, also benefit at the time?

Is all of this merely coincidence, or were the explorations of the human race carried on the backs of wolves?

The notch through the granite ridge, where the hunter found his caribou,

still exists near Ravenwood. Though the caribou are gone, white-tailed deer travel through the ravine. In the woods, wolves wait for them. Hunters still use dogs in much the same manner as our ancestors did.

We have been predators for millions of years. We have not changed much, either in form or passion. Much has been written about how we have changed the dog, scientists claiming that the range of aberrant human behaviors is mirrored in what has become of our canine companions. This, too, I question. Having lived with dogs all my life and having observed wolves for much of my life, I see the wolf in the dog and the dog in the wolf. The more I think about it, the fewer differences I see between the two.

I have had serene, peaceful, wild wolves sit ten feet from me, confident and trusting. These are qualities we cherish in a dog. I have also seen the wild counterpart of the nervous, high-strung dog—wolves that pace, that are nervous, that flinch at noises or challenges. Dogs are generally calmer; wolves react to almost everything, but the depth of both behaviors is the same.

We've selected the calmer dogs for domestication, so they are more common than they would be in the wild, but some are no more relaxed than a calm wolf. It would make sense that we would only be able to tame the calmer wolves; the nervous wolves would have kept their distance. We still try to avoid owning nervous dogs, but they reflect the sensitivity of the wolf.

THE SHOWY LADY'S SLIPPER ORCHID, COMMON AT RAVENWOOD.

We cherish the dog for its companionship. Dogs seem almost to read our minds; they react to our unhappiness and our joy. It does not diminish the comfort of that companionship to understand that their "sixth sense" is the astute ability to read our body language—the same skill wolves use to establish pack hierarchy through posturing. That we can so love another species, mourning them at their death and missing them in their absence, speaks volumes about human compassion. It also says much about the dog. I have seen native people who evidenced little love toward the dogs they used as work animals, particularly in the far north before the advent of the snowmobile, but I do not think that the love we show for individual dogs is a modern invention. The burial site in Israel indicates the possibility of early, cherished companionship. Dogs being dogs and humans being humans, it is inconceivable that affectionate bonds did not spring up long ago.

Think also of our most respected and cherished dogs: seeing-eye and guard dogs. They evidence the same intelligence and skills that prompted us to adopt the wolf. The use of a seeing-eye Labrador's senses, though different in purpose, is not far from an early hunter's use of his wolf to help him explore a wild world. And the guard dog, whether a mongrel roaming a junkyard or a German shepherd partnered with a human police officer, is not unlike the wolf that protected our caves. Our faith in such dogs surely began with an early trust in the wolf/dog.

Make no mistake. A wolf is not a dog. There have been changes in temperament over the long ages, and I don't condone attempts to tame wolves as pets—nor do I favor intentional wolf-dog hybrids. There is no need to repeat the long process of domestication, and in any event it cannot be redone over a few generations or through hybridization. I can't deny the exhilaration of the thought of relating to, and living with, the pristine intellect of the wolf that motivates those people who would own a wolf or a hybrid. But too often these tame wolves or hybrids turn into sad stories: big animals, sometimes a bit too aggressive, that owners weary of and put to sleep or cage. Some even try to release these unfortunate animals in the wild, where they perish or turn to killing livestock, the depredation then blamed on wolves.

Though the wolf is not a dog, the dog is some kind of wolf. I believe it resulted from an ancient pact made when both species were young, when the land was virginal and the lust of life in the wild ran deeply through both races. The dog is a reminder of that covenant. Its primal passion lies just beneath its skin, nearer the surface than our own. But we still share it. Some part of us remembers the passion, and remembers our indebtedness.

We have been partners with the wolf for almost as long as we have been successful as a tool-using race. Now the wolf that so many have hated sits at the hearth of a neighbor, wearing a collar and chewing a rawhide toy. One can only wonder why we have come to hate and fear Brother Wolf, especially when we so love and cherish the dog. There is a sense of bigotry about it.

Is it because Brother Wolf reminds us of the ancient, forgotten promise?

PACKS CAN HEAR A HOWLING WOLF FROM FIVE MILES AWAY.

one hundred seven

The remains of the white-tailed deer lay scattered in the autumn bracken, like glass at the scene of an accident. How I had missed it on my previous wanderings I'll never know, because I'd been through this area many times since the deer had met its demise the previous winter. On this chill fall day, with the wind rattling the last seared leaves of the aspen trees, I stooped over the grey remains.

I studied the evidence like a forensic pathologist. Bones, crushed in order to get at the nutritious marrow, clearly indicated a wolf kill. Tufts of deer hair were scattered about, tossed by wolves and wind. If there had been no hair at the site, I might have had trouble determining which species had died here, for the few bones were broken like shards, making identification difficult. The skull was missing; it had probably been carted off at the time of the kill or soon afterward.

The hill where the deer died is a ten-minute walk behind my cabin. The incline is steep, and it slopes down to a clear wilderness lake. I stood there among the aspens and jack pines and studied the scene, trying to reconstruct just what had happened on this granite grade. Playing woods detective is a

favorite pastime of mine, going back to my boyhood on the prairie, when I'd studied tracks in the snow.

I surveyed the scene without moving. As the sun peeked through the sooty, snow-filled clouds for a moment, its warmth stroked my face, and I realized the significance of this south-facing slope. In winter, south slopes are the favorite places of animals, deer included. They pause here to gather the sun's wan warmth into their cold coats. Cedars grew at the base of this slope, along the granite shoreline, so a deer walking on the ice could feed on branches that swept over the lake. If the kill took place in late winter, the first warmth of spring might have melted the snow away on this slope, attracting the deer to the unveiled foods. For one or more of these reasons, the deer may have come to the scene of its death.

No one will ever know if the deer ran far before it was caught that day, or if it had been ambushed as it napped in the sun or browsed on the cedars. Was it sick and starving after a long winter? Did the wolves have an easy time of it? Or was it a chase of desperation, going a great distance as the deer bounded in 12-foot leaps until it could bound no longer, the wolves running silently, their great splayed feet punching the snow, their tongues lolling with the taste of anticipation and the heat of the chase?

It stuns some people to realize that such scenes take place. There is a sense of brutality to it. Perhaps this is why some do not like wolves. Others simply ignore the reality of prey and predator, choosing to believe that the wilderness is some mythical, peaceable kingdom.

When I am away from Ravenwood and my mind drifts to the dark forests, when my spirit wanders the trails, I think of what is happening there—of the life-and-death struggle that unfolds daily. From the sheltered world of "civilization," we can scarcely comprehend the rhythm of nature, the recycling of nutrients, the interdependence of all life. "All meat is grass," the old saying goes. It is true. The prey eat the grass. The carnivores eat the prey, and when the predators die, they become grass. And a million other things.

Take, for instance, the bone I found at this particular site—a bone gnawed by mice. I suppose the mice were drawn to it by the minerals locked within. The minerals had been extracted from the soil through the grass that had been eaten by the deer; the deer had become bone that found its way inside the mice; the mice may have ended up inside an owl; and the owl would return to the soil upon its death.

Nature is a cycle in which all things are really everything else. The most dramatic part of this cycle, the death of an animal (we rarely mourn the death of a plant) occurs frequently, whether we are aware of it or not and whether we like it or not. There is immense drama in nature, a drama of fleeting existence and mortality revealed. Everything eats. Everything is eaten.

I got to my knees and searched through the deer's remains for tidbits. As I turned over a patch of deer hair, a button popped out. A button? I picked it

Perched on antlers, a diminutive black-capped chickadee waits its turn. Ravens with four-foot wingspans swoop down to inspect the carcass of a whitetail deer, later bringing morsels to their young in the nest. No food is wasted in the woods. Death feeds life in a cycle of renewal that is necessary, though sometimes hard for modern humans to accept.

up. Black with a grey rim, the button looked like an archer's target. I turned it over. Suddenly I realized this was no man-made item.

It was an eye, nearly petrified. From which creature had this dime-sized eye come? I thought of all the animals in the forest. I wondered which ones had visited this site, and which would have been attracted to a deer carcass. I thought of all the animal eyes I have ever looked into through a spotting scope or a camera lens. Of course!

The eye was a raven's eye. I knelt, dumbfounded. Ravens are wise. They are also immensely cautious. Something must have caught and killed this raven, but what? Wolves and ravens often interact at kill sites, but they do so with little or no animosity. Coyotes sometimes try to catch ravens, but a coyote would have eaten the entire bird, digesting the eye. Something small and swift must have caught this most foolish raven.

It was a marten, or maybe a fisher, I guessed. I've often seen both around Ravenwood, and I've seen them come to dine on the scraps of a wolf kill. Perhaps, as the raven fed on the carcass, a marten lunged with its weasel's speed at the glossy black bird. It must have sunk its teeth into a vulnerable spot in order to down such a powerful bird.

I picked up bits of bone, deer hair, and raven feathers, and tucked them with the eye into my pocket. These pieces of woods memories would become artifacts for my "nature altar" back at the cabin. Though I had walked into the drama well after the final curtain had descended, I knew the performance would be given time and time again.

Clunk . . . One thousand fourteen, one thousand fifteen. *Clunk.* Every 15 seconds, a pine cone dropped into my blind. I stared up at the red squirrel that was dropping the cones with annoying accuracy. A movement caught my eye and I turned to my task, which was watching a bear carcass that lay across the ravine from me. The ravens were getting excited.

I didn't know how the bear had died. It might have been hit by a car on a nearby road, then crawled off to die; or it might have been shot by a resort owner. Black bears had been plentiful near settlements and dwellings this year because of a failed berry crop. Resort owners sometimes intentionally gut-shoot a bear that becomes a nuisance. The wound is fatal, but not immediately so. The bear wanders off to die instead of dropping dead in the parking lot, which saves some explaining when the game warden comes around to investigate.

Before I discovered this bear, I'd found bear hair lodged in wolf scat, so this was not the first bear to die nearby this autumn. The bear that was eaten by the wolves may have been shot first, or it may have been killed by the wolves. Canadian researcher Paul Paquette, working in Manitoba, documented three black bear kills by a wolf pack in the course of just one winter, including instances in which the bears were dug up and dragged out of their

A PINE MARTEN PICKS AT A DEER RIB CAGE.

WHITETAIL DOES, EVER-ALERT TO PREDATORS.

one hundred fifteen

Ravens puzzle over entry into a thick-skinned bear carcass.

dens. One winter I found sign where a pack of wolves had dug a hibernating bear (and perhaps newborn cubs) out of an abandoned beaver lodge.

The bear in the ravine, though, was not killed by wolves, nor even visited by them. Not yet, at any rate. I watched patiently in the hope that the wolves would come.

Actually, I was confident they would come. The ravens had discovered the carcass the day before, and today they were already in the trees at dawn, when I awoke to resume my watch. Others came quickly, their black, glossy feathers gleaming in the sunlight, rowing with their four-foot wings in whooshes above the forest. When they came to the site of the carcass, some would flutter into a tree; others would tip sideways, spilling air from beneath their wings and plummeting to the ground a few yards from the bear. They were yelling, one after another, as if to say, "Come, wolves. We're afraid! Help us out." The wolves, I knew, would hear.

At the moment, the carcass was too formidable for the ravens to feed upon. A bear in its prime, like this one, is fat, with tough, elastic skin. Since the carcass was intact, the ravens found little to eat. Their tugs at the skin resulted only in beaks full of hair—hardly a satisfying meal.

Today, for a long time, no raven was brave enough to approach the bear. Finally, as day hurried toward dusk, two gun-metal blue ravens sat on the bear's paws, which were stretched in front of and to each side of the animal's head, as if it had died in mid-leap.

The two birds began pecking at the bear's eyes.

I've seen a lot of things in the woods, but my stomach turned as I watched the ravens eat the eyes with obvious relish, then clean the sockets, thrusting their sharp beaks into the cavities. The bear had a particularly empty look on its face by the time the birds were done.

I considered the bear's dignity, or lack of it, as it lay sprawled under the white pines, being eaten bit by bit and ounce by ounce. Nature, I suppose, has little regard for dignity. By dark, no wolves had arrived, and I hoped they would stay away until the next day, so I could photograph them. I busied myself at the cabin that evening, restless with anticipation.

Bernd Heinrich, who wrote a fascinating book called *Ravens in Winter* about the raven research he conducted in the woods of Maine, found little correlation between the ravens' recruitment call (the "yell," as he called it) and the eventual arrival of predators. This surprised me. Ravens use the call to attract each other, but it is my feeling that they also call to attract predators—especially wolves—to unopened carcasses. I can only speculate that my experience is different from Heinrich's because wolves are not present in Maine, or because ravens relate differently to predators here than they do in Maine. But I have repeatedly seen wolves, as well as coyotes, come to a carcass shortly after it was discovered by yelling ravens.

The advantage for the ravens in this case, of course, was evident. With no means of penetrating the bear's thick skin, the ravens could not easily gain access to the meat. Wolves could rip the carcass open, for their own benefit and ultimately for the benefit of the ravens. After all, a piece of something is better than all of nothing.

The advantage for wolves or coyotes of heeding the raven's cry almost goes without saying. It results in meat. Even humans respond to the calling of ravens and travel to see what the birds have found. I've done so numerous times, and found treasures of wolf-prey encounters.

Local game warden Al Heidebrink tells me that the raven is one of a warden's most useful tools in finding the remains of animals killed by poachers. Some poachers go to the extreme of dousing the remains with kerosene. The ravens, which find the carcass and realize it is not edible, do not call; without the ruckus, the warden is less likely to discover the kill. Early humans must have used the raven for the similar purpose of locating a meal.

The ravens seemed particularly nervous around this bear carcass. Ravens on the ground always approach a carcass nervously, often "pogoing" into the air with a flap of their wings, as if to test whether the animal is truly dead, hoping to elicit a response if it is alive. There is a sense of braggadocio to some ravens' approach as they sidestep up to the carcass in a nonchalant manner,

only to peck quickly, then jump away and strut, like fat businessmen in black suits. This behavior has occurred at every kill I've monitored, and it continues until the carcass is certified harmless by the settling in of one bold raven or the presence of wolves. When the animal is verified dead, the entire flock moves in. I've seen as many as 70 ravens feeding on the same deer.

The ravens' routine is usually predictable. One or two birds (they sometimes fly in mated pairs, and they mate for life) discover a carcass. After some nervous testing, one bird begins yelling to attract more ravens—or perhaps wolves, if the carcass is intact. When large numbers of ravens gather on a carcass, they can consume an enormous amount of meat—an amount often wrongly attributed to wolves. By the time they are finished, the bones are so clean they nearly shine.

Though it would seem counter-productive to invite others to consume food you've just found, doing so is an aid to survival in the raven's world. The presence of more birds means more watchful eyes and noise-sensitive ears. This is the same safety-in-numbers strategy practiced by grazing animals such as elk or bison, and even by grazing birds such as Canada geese. Gatherings around a carcass also seem to serve a social purpose. I've seen many courtship displays while ravens were scavenging.

The efficiency of ravens at a carcass encourages wolves to engorge themselves. Able to consume as much as twenty pounds at one meal—one quarter of their average weight—wolves take full advantage of their relatively infrequent

EXCITED RAVEN CALLS MAY DRAW OPPORTUNISTIC WOLVES.

one hundred nineteen

meals. If they did not, they might return to a kill a few hours later to find that ravens and other scavengers had stripped it clean.

Dawn and the ravens had both arrived, and I had a feeling from the start that this would be a big day. The morning's activity around the bear reinforced my theory that the greater the perceived danger (a bear is seen as more dangerous than a deer), the more showing off occurs for the benefit of other ravens.

Now many of the birds, though not yet perched on the carcass, strut around it with their feathered neck bibs fluffed to fullness and their "ears"—tall ridges of feathers on both temples—erect. Often two or three ravens strut toward the carcass, side by side, with an air of cockiness that makes them resemble street toughs hogging a sidewalk.

A light snow begins to fall. There are ravens in the trees and on the ground, but none on the impenetrable carcass. Suddenly, as the pace of the snow quickens, those ravens on the ground fly into the trees. I look around.

A wolf has appeared on the ridge.

If I thought the ravens had been nervous, this wolf puts them to shame. It trots in cautiously, downwind of the bear, and crouches on its front paws. It repeatedly looks up at the ravens. Ever so slowly, the wolf works toward the

bear, then finally gives it a timid nip before leaping back. The bear does not move. This encourages the wolf, which more boldly moves in for a second nip. Again, the bear does not move. The wolf looks up at the ravens, looks all around the forest, then takes a serious bite out of the bear. Like leaves falling from trees, the ravens tumble down to the bear.

This wolf is alone, but judging from its demeanor, I'd say it has good status within its pack. I say this because I think ravens have some understanding of wolf "body language," and so they react to individual wolves differently. Wolves that display clear dominance are pestered less often by the ravens. On the other hand, wolves that approach with a submissive air are sometimes subjected to dive bombings and peckings. It seems obvious that ravens know when they can get away with misbehaving, for they do not test all wolves—only those that are likely to tolerate it. They may even be acquainted personally with the wolf, having shared many experiences within their mutual range.

In this instance, all feed together. The wolf grabs a chunk and steps back to eat it, then the ravens step onto the carcass and peck at the newly exposed flesh. As I watch, the ravens peel back the bear's fatty skin, stuffing chunks of white fat into their beaks. As the flesh is cleaned, they tug the skin back further, rolling it under their feet like we would roll up a carpet.

Once the wolf has opened the carcass, the ravens are quite capable of finishing the job. In fact, I've seen situations in which the ravens consumed more of a

A RED FOX—THE WOLF'S SMALLER RELATIVE.

THE SNOWSHOE HARE IS THE MAIN PREY OF THE CANADA LYNX.

one hundred twenty-three

BALD EAGLES FIGHT FOR POSSESSION OF CARRION.

one hundred twenty-four

deer than the wolves. A couple of times, this wolf appears annoyed by the birds, dashing halfheartedly toward them and flushing them into the trees.

On a different occasion, I filmed an aggressive, dominant, nearly black wolf as it grabbed and shook a raven. The raven must have managed to peck the wolf, for it quickly dropped the bird and the raven flew away. In an act that I can only call "showing off," ravens sometimes approach feeding wolves from behind and peck at them, then dodge out of range. They also pull on the tail feathers of bald eagles that sometimes join ravens at a carcass.

Their behavior reminds me of a Plains Indians practice known as "counting coup," in which a warrior on foot or on horseback strikes an enemy with a stick. The exercise affords honor to the warrior, but leaves no dead enemy to mourn. Something similar goes on with ravens. I also filmed one hanging upside down from a spindly branch above a feeding wolf, like some giant nuthatch. It then dropped to the ground and lay on its back in the snow, feet up, peering over its shoulder at the other ravens, almost flaunting its bravery by ignoring the wolf so very near.

Perhaps ravens perform such acts to demonstrate their own status within the flock, to attract mates, or to reaffirm their desirability to their selected mate. These are very intelligent birds. Today I watch as one raven cleans bear fat off its beak by sticking its bill into a punky piece of birch. One bird, sitting atop the bear, repeatedly opens its bill and thrusts morsels of fat in and out with its tongue, again as if showing off. Another raven, flying off with a bit of meat, lands near the brook and begins to hop on the ground, inspecting everything. Time and again, it rolls a rock or a leaf over. Finally, it caches the piece of meat under a leaf, arranging the leaf to suit itself. Then it places more leaves atop the meat, flies up to a branch, and looks down. It must see

something it doesn't like, because it jumps down and repeats the whole process until it is satisfied that the morsel is well hidden.

Caching of food is a common practice among both ravens and wolves. With their keen eyesight and their "overview" of the landscape, I would expect that ravens often find and devour the wolves' carefully hidden caches. I've proven this to myself by caching morsels in a wolf-like manner, as carefully as I could, only to find later that the food was gone. Raven tracks were evident.

At another kill, I watched a raven grab a bone that the wolves had broken, standing the bone upright by pushing the unbroken end into the snow. With the marrow thus presented, the raven leisurely sipped as far into the bone as it could reach with its beak. Such behavior amounts almost to the use of tools.

While I can often distinguish individual wolves by their size, color, and manner, raven study is hindered by the fact they are all virtually identical. Young ravens can be distinguished from old ones by the pink lining of their mouths (older birds' mouths are lined with black); and an individual bird will occasionally display particular characteristics. But this happens rarely. Today I'm fortunate—one of the ravens feeding on the bear has white, scaly feet and legs. It looks as if it is wearing spats.

Native Americans, especially those from the Pacific Northwest, revered the raven and placed it at the center of much mythology. Raven is known as a trickster and a creator, and ravens are almost always the top figure on totem poles.

It is easy to understand the native peoples' fascination with the raven. Though I've studied wolves and ravens on and off for ten years at Ravenwood, the birds are no less suspicious of me than they were during our first encounters. Since ravens can live to be 40 years old, they have a long time in which to accumulate wisdom, and I can state unequivocally that, at a kill site, ravens are more suspicious and alert than wolves. In many instances, I have seen ravens become nervous at one of my small movements while the wolves seemed unaware. I believe that the birds serve the wolves as extra eyes and ears.

In all the popular literature I've read on ravens, there is only a rare mention of wolves. Yet here in northern Minnesota, the two seem inseparable. Durward Allen, the noted early researcher who studied the wolf packs of Isle Royale National Park in Lake Superior, remarked in his studies that ravens always seem to be in the company of wolves. Native peoples, especially the Inuit, assert that ravens actually accompany wolves on their travels and hunts. Another researcher who specialized in wolf vocalizations, Fred Harrington, indicated that ravens will come to a wolf's howl.

All of which makes sense. Only a foolish wolf would fail to check out the cause of a commotion caused by ravens. Likewise, only a silly raven would ignore the possibility of a meal when wolves are howling about a hunt. These reactions are indicative of intelligence, but they don't necessarily indicate language. They might instead represent a Pavlovian sort of conditioned response. Dogs fed on canned dog food will appear immediately when they hear the whir of an electric can opener. The wolf, no less intelligent, could certainly associate the calling of ravens with the prospect of food. And ravens, I believe, are quite capable of learning the benefit of seeking out wolves.

On occasion, while howling to locate a wolf pack, I've had ravens fly to me. One of my untested ideas is to broadcast the recorded sounds of ravens at a carcass. I suspect that wolves would eventually come to the commotion. Since ravens produce about 250 vocalizations, it also seems likely that wolves can discern those nuances that are beneficial to them—such as a feeding call—from those that are not. Is this a form of cross-species communication that approximates language in its crudest sense?

There is yet another connection between the two species. Allen noted, and I concur, that wolves and ravens seem to play together. He reported instances in which wolves and ravens played a game of "tag" on the frozen lakes of Isle Royale. I've seen similar interactions.

I believe ravens enjoy the company of wolves, and that they tease and play with wolves as a means of making an impression on their flock. Many intelligent birds, such as crows and parrots, need toys and stimulation, and perhaps wolves provide stimulation for ravens. I can think of no other reason why a raven will fly to a wolf that is not in the presence of food.

Native people speculate that ravens lead wolves to food, and this does not strike me as farfetched. I'm convinced that this does occur in the case of an

A RAVEN TORMENTS AN UNYIELDING EAGLE.

DEFYING DANGER, THE TRICKSTER RAVEN PECKS AT A FOOT.

one hundred twenty-seven

unopened carcass. And a raven armed with the knowledge that wolves can open a carcass might also begin to give a recruitment call when it spots living prey. What has it got to lose? If the wolves come and are successful, the raven benefits tremendously for its small effort. And think of the advantage for wolves of having "aerial reconnaissance." The pairing of the two species would be an efficient one, and they could function almost as one living organism.

It is no insult to my game warden friends to say that they are no more intelligent than our hunting ancestors. And if wardens wisely use the crafty raven to find the poachers' spoils, early humans must certainly have learned that a raven might lead them to food. When we adopted the wolf/dog that hunted for us, we may also have discovered its lingering association with ravens. If we wounded an animal that was able to run a great distance before our wolves brought it down, perhaps the calling of the attendant ravens would lead us to the animal.

I have found wolf packs around my territory by watching the swooping of ravens (they often dive above a pack) or by listening to their calls. Over the years, my ears learned to recognize the distinctive voice of ravens in the presence of their partners, the wolves. Ravens, after all, are busybodies. They know everything that is happening in the woods—and by eavesdropping on the eavesdroppers, I become better informed.

Ravens even share the wolf's bad reputation. The term "ravenous" didn't stem from positive feelings about ravens. And, during the constant squabbles of our violent race, both wolves and ravens have fed upon our battlefield dead—leading to a host of medieval horror stories. My own great-grandfather, Ole Andreasen, died trying to release a log jam below Kvellans Falls on the mountain river Lynga, near Lyngdal, in his native Norway. He was found in 1904 by his neighbor Samuel Sorlid, who followed the raven calls to the spot where the body lay frozen in ice. Neighbor Sorlid evidently knew the language of the great black bird. My Grandmother Otelia Aanenson was a young girl when this tragedy took place and remembered it well. She vividly retold this story to me several times during my growing-up years.

In an odd way, it seems fitting that my great-grandfather, son of Vikings, was found by ravens. Vikings were known to carry ravens on their ocean journeys, where the birds were released at sea. Thus, men were led to land by ravens that spotted it from aloft. Odin, the All-Father of Norse mythology, even perched a raven upon each shoulder. After they flew over the world each day, Odin's companions Hugin and Munin (Thought and Memory), returned to whisper the world's events into his ears.

It is unfortunate that we apply our own moral standards in deciding which animals are good and which are bad. Of course, animals are neither. They simply are. We practice species (and specious) discrimination when we judge animals according to our own predilections. They are all part of one system. They can't be separated from that system and analyzed based on how they fit our moral standards. If the raven and the wolf have been unjustly branded as "bad" in much of the world, it is comforting to realize that at least some peoples have regarded these creatures as teachers and partners.

When the wolves leave a carcass to once again stalk the quiet forest, a succession of creatures appears. Martens and fishers set upon clean ribs in order to chew leftover bits. Lushly coated foxes find fragments of food.

Coyotes, which often bark angrily in the distance until the wolves leave, sneak in for a snack. Eagles join the ravens in thoroughly stripping the carcass. Naked-headed turkey vultures ugly up for a meal. Hairy and downy woodpeckers trade birch trees for backbones. Even the flittering chickadees and the acrobatic nuthatches descend with the Canada jays for dinner.

Eventually, in spring, the mice, voles, insects, and microbes turn what is left of the carcass into new life. The enriched soil pushes up new growth that will one day be eaten by a deer, which will itself be eaten. So, although ravens have a special relationship with the wolves, all of the forest occupants benefit from the chase and kill.

This is the cornerstone of ecology—the understanding that, at some level, all creatures are dependent upon each other. Others have written eloquently on this subject, and I'm sure it is not new to most readers. But it seems that we have only recently rediscovered the concept. Only through the efforts of great thinkers such as Aldo Leopold have our eyes been reopened. Here are Leopold's words, excerpted from *Round River:*

The outstanding scientific discovery of the twentieth century is not television, or radio, but rather the complexity of the land organism. The last word in ignorance is the man who says of an animal or plant: "What good is it?" If the land mechanism as a whole is good, then every part is good, whether we understand it or not. If the biota, in the course of aeons, has built something we like but do not understand, then who but a fool would discard seemingly useless parts? To keep every cog and wheel is the first precaution of intelligent tinkering.

In our attempts to save the bigger cogs and wheels, we are still pretty naive. A little repentance just before a species goes over the brink is enough to make us feel virtuous. When the species is gone we have a good cry and repeat the performance.

Nature's intricacy is difficult to fathom. But the vaults of ecological understanding must be opened to those who value only the green that fits in their wallets. In many ways, this is the central challenge of our time.

As I wander Ravenwood, I see interdependencies occurring daily. We have witnessed these lessons since we first could think. We are not merely observers, but participants in the process. We benefit as each animal benefits. Despite all the things that we are, we remain part of the natural cycle. But too often, we forget.

The wolves, the ravens, and the deer function almost as one organism. Ravenwood itself functions like one large living thing. Its trees are lungs, its water is blood, and the thousands of creatures that live and die upon it are the very cells of the living world.

The wolf has been our companion. It certainly was our teacher. As a vital part of a fully functioning ecosystem, the wolf can again serve as teacher, reminding us that two species sharing similar ecological niches might also share similar fates.

If, one day, the wolf no longer finds the world a fit place in which to live, we may face a similar and inescapable destiny.

WOLVES CAN EXPLODE INTO ACTION.

WOLVES AND HUMAN NATURE

I could hear them plainly now on both sides of the river, could hear the brush crack as they hurdled windfalls in their path. When I heard the full-throated bawling howl, I should have had chills racing up and down my spine. Instead, I was thrilled to know that the big grays might have picked up my trail and were following me down the glistening frozen highway of the river.

When Sigurd Olson wrote these words in 1945, as part of an essay about wolves in his book, *The Singing Wilderness*, he was truly ahead of his time. The passage reveals a man who, long before most of his contemporaries, began to understand the value and beauty of wolves.

For those unfamiliar with his work, let me explain that Sigurd is virtually synonymous with the lake country around Ravenwood. He began a long struggle in the 1920s to preserve and protect this region, as well as the canoe country that is now the Boundary Waters Canoe Area Wilderness and Quetico Provincial Park. He succeeded at long last, and his books fostered environmental consciousness in tens of thousands of people at a time when environmentalism was a foreign concept to most. Coincidentally, the protection of the ecosystem also meant protection of the wolf, for in this largely

roadless land, the Minnesota wolf held its ground.

Sigurd Olson lived for most of his life in Ely, Minnesota, where he was vilified by neighbors and townspeople for his pro-wilderness and pro-wolf beliefs. But, like many other people, he had at one time despised wolves.

In "The Poison Trail," published in the December 1930 edition of *Sports Afield* magazine, Olson chronicles his 100-mile winter journey with trappers. Along a trail of death, government-sponsored trappers had spread poison baits. Time and again, Olson and his friends collected the carcasses of wolves, coyotes, and foxes that died an almost-instant death when they consumed the bait. Throughout his story, Olson refers to the wolves as "grey marauders" and "killers," and as "savage-looking brutes" that had been out "murdering."

For those of us who admire the wolf, the story is difficult to read. If we are familiar with Olson's later essays, it is even more distressing. How could a beloved teacher, a fine writer, and an enlightened thinker rejoice at the death of wolves?

Careful readers, though, can discern Olson's early distress at the ecological cost of such poisoning. He expresses little remorse over the death of wolves, but he questions the loss of non-targeted species that also succumbed to the bait. His concern would lead him to pose further and deeper questions—questions that would not be answered by the villainous myths surrounding the wolf. Like Aldo Leopold, whose early professional years were spent

destroying wolves, Olson soon reached a philosophical impasse.

He must—and he would—arrive at his own answers.

Sigurd Olson undertook one of the first studies of wolves in their natural habitat. His landmark study, published in 1938, was the first to document the wolf's family unit and its complex social structure, and his insights led other researchers to ask many more questions.

Sig Olson had opened the windows so the fresh air of new attitudes could enter. Ely, Minnesota, once a hotbed of wolf hostility, now paints wolf tracks on the sidewalks to lead customers to retailers' doors. Even the *Ely Echo*, the town's newspaper, sports a wolf paw print logo on its masthead.

Ten years ago, I couldn't get the U.S. Postal Service to issue a wolf postage stamp. But in 1993, a portion of my wolf video was used as a large-screen background during President Clinton's inauguration festivities in Washington. Movies like *Never Cry Wolf* and *Dances With Wolves* have popularized the animal in a manner that few could have foreseen. Our attitudes are changing. But the struggle to understand and live in peace with the wolf is not over.

Some people continue to cling to the traditional myth, holding that wolves embody evil; others have woven new myths about the wolf, depicting it as a

RAVENWOOD'S THICK BOREAL FOREST.

YOUNG WOLVES RESPOND TO THE HOWLS OF ADULTS.

one hundred thirty-five

spiritual guide that must be protected at every turn, or as a lovable, Disneyesque animal just one step removed from domestication.

Whatever their intentions, myths are myths. When they are mistaken for literal reality, they obscure the truth and make it difficult for people to understand each other. They create divisions.

Here is a telling irony. At this writing, the state of Alaska has been under attack for announcing a plan that would remove up to 80 percent of the wolves from three game management areas within the state. Alaskan officials claim the wolf removal plan will lead to an increase in the size of moose and caribou herds. At best, this is extremely poor game management; in reality, it appears that those in power simply want an excuse to practice some old-fashioned wolf persecution.

As Alaska contemplates killing wolves for nonsensical reasons, other people within the same nation struggle to reintroduce wolves to a region from which we have only recently eliminated them. In the American West, only Montana now contains a viable, reproducing population of wolves. These wolves reside north of Yellowstone, in and near Glacier National Park. The proposed reintroduction of wolves to Yellowstone National Park has been controversial. Ranchers in the area issue dire warnings about the dangers of returning the "killer wolf" to public lands; on the other hand, environmental groups like Defenders of Wildlife have tirelessly pressured the federal government to implement a reintroduction program.

While the battle is being fought, the wolves may simply return to Yellowstone on their own. A photographer working in the park recently filmed a large, wolf-like animal feeding on a carcass alongside a grizzly bear. I've seen the film, and I believe the animal was a wolf. No captive wolf or hybrid would have fed so confidently so near a grizzly, nor utterly ignored the coyote that sat and watched. Some wolf researchers have claimed that the animal filmed was not a wolf, but a hybrid. Some of the scientists, I believe, actually do not wish to see the wolf successful of its own accord. If the wolf returns to Yellowstone on its own, it would mean an end to some researchers' professional meddling and tinkering. Along with ecology, job security seems to be at stake. In any event, it seems likely that the wolves, acting on their own impulses, will soon establish a breeding population within the most famous national park in the U.S.

This is as it should be. Wolves know what is best for them, and they know how to do what they do best. They will hunt, breed, and establish territories without our help. The only thing they need from us is our restraint while they establish themselves. Nature inevitably does a better job than science, and the wolf will undoubtedly prove once again that it can get along without our interference.

Growth is one of the most important attributes of the human spirit. Sigurd Olson grew and changed; he helped others experience similar growth. In all of today's attention to wolves, I see a weather vane turning in

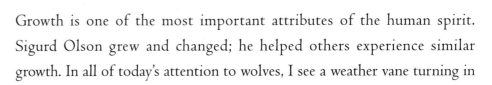

a new wind and pointing in a new direction, reflecting the magnitude of our shifting mood. Many of us now respect and learn from other animals. But even enlightened thinkers like Olson and Leopold did not come to their conclusions overnight; and, like the trees, we all grow at different rates. Those who have been taught to fear and despise the wolf cannot change without time, effort, and the will to redefine their relationship with these intelligent animals.

For each of us who values wolves, there are many, many more people who simply struggle to stay alive and to make their way in this world. Whenever human needs come into conflict with the wolf, we will be tested. If population pressures push humans into the wolf's space, or if wolf populations spread into human space, the wolf may suffer. But if we come to see wolves in their true light, then hope exists for both species.

Wolves and humans can learn to live together in the modern world. Consider what has happened in Minnesota. State and federal agencies there have worked to increase the number of wolves living in the state as part of a wolf recovery program initiated when the wolf was fully protected in 1974. At that time, about 1,000 wolves lived in Minnesota. At this writing, they number close to 2,000—and they have spread to Wisconsin and Michigan's Upper Peninsula, where they are reestablishing themselves.

It should be mentioned here that with the expansion of wolf populations, problems occur. It is easy to be smug about a wolf killing a cow—unless it

is *your* cow. However, proven livestock killers are removed in order to ensure that the race of wolves, most of which do not kill livestock, can find peace with humans. In Minnesota, farmers are compensated for their livestock losses and problem wolves are destroyed—a process that has allowed wolves to increase fourfold in 20 years. Farmer education has also helped solve some problems.

There is almost insurmountable evidence that living with wolves does not have to be controversial; nor need it be an either/or situation. Though the tensions between people and wolves have not disappeared in Minnesota, enough headway has been made to allow wolves to flourish. Can wolves and humans coexist?

The answer is clear: We can.

The deeper truth is even clearer: We must.

In the narrows, the spruces stood tall and black against the sky. The shores there were only a stone's throw apart. I must walk straight down the center, must not run, must not break my pace; and suddenly I was aware that, in spite of reason and my knowledge of the predators, ancient reactions were coming to the fore, intuitive warnings out of the past. In spite of what I knew, I was responding to the imagined threat of the narrows, like a Stone Age hunter cut off from his cave.

—Sigurd Olson, The Singing Wilderness

CONFIDENCE AND INTELLIGENCE ARE SIGNS OF A FUTURE PACK LEADER.

Sigurd Olson's description of snowshoeing down a dark and frozen river captures the unreasoning fear that overtook him when he sensed that wolves were very near. It is a fear we all possess. The difference between those who will live with wolves and those who will not is that the latter allow their fear to dominate their reason.

Wolves are not to be unduly feared. There has been no verified attack on humans by a healthy wolf in North America. Not one. But, even knowing this, it is hard to suppress the ancient reflex.

I have felt the same fear during the blue-black of a winter evening deep in the forest of Ravenwood. The starkness of winter, and the knowledge that everything in the frigid forest is eking out an existence, makes the world seem scarier and more desperate. As Olson points out in the same essay, if a wolf chose to attack a human, the struggle would be short and unevenly matched. When I watch wolves rip apart a kill, when I see the power in their straining haunches and the terrible tearing teeth, it is difficult not to imagine myself in the prey's position. But in all my wolf encounters, I've only felt threatened once, and in that instance I was at fault.

Several years ago, I was attempting to film an alpha male, Buster, that had discovered a dead, beached seal on Ellesmere Island. As the wolf ate, I sat frustrated because the entire scene was cast in shadows, and I knew my footage would be unusable. After a while, the wolf wandered off. I seized the opportunity, moved down to the carcass, and dragged it into the wonderful Arctic sunlight.

Preoccupied with my task, I was at first unaware that the wolf had returned. When I looked up, I was instantly frightened. I'd seen his

A CANADA JAY INSPECTS THE AFTERMATH OF A DEADLY BATTLE.

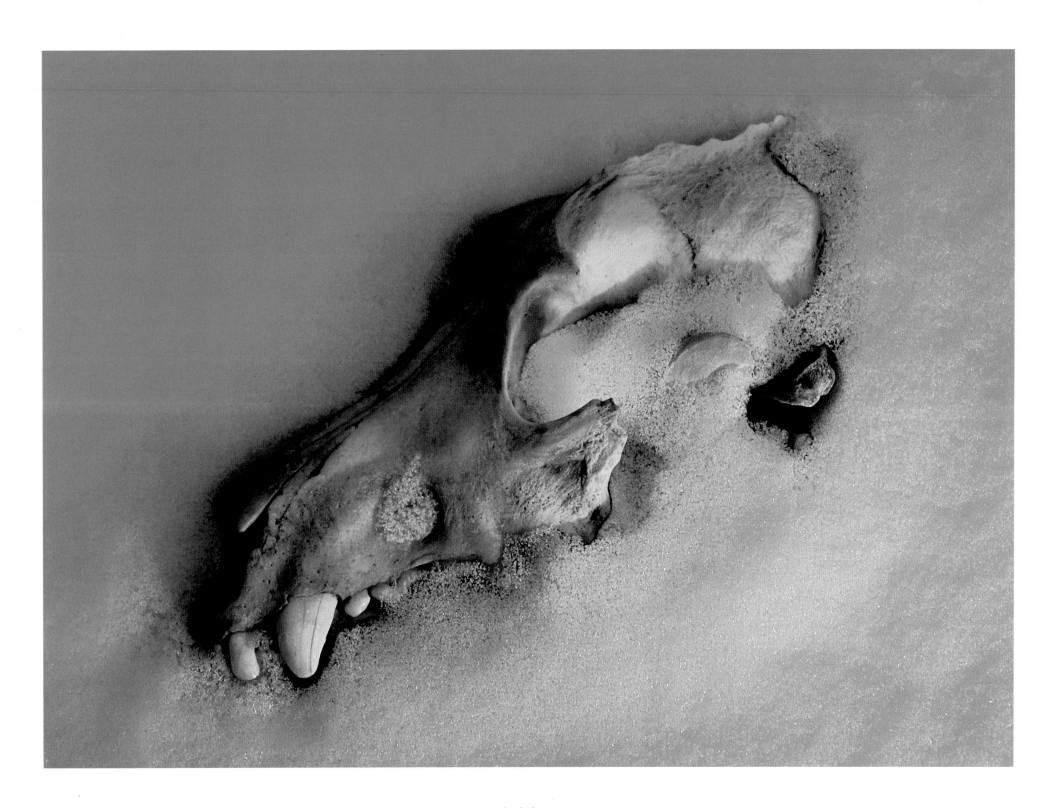

"aggressive" posture when he dealt with other wolves, and I could tell he was unhappy with me for apparently trying to make off with his seal.

Every hair was erect on the wolf's back, and those on the back of my neck rose in response. Because wolves so readily read body language, I think they see our normal erect posture as a sign of dominance. But in this case I was crouched over the seal, a posture the wolf may have interpreted as submissive behavior.

The wolf came running toward me, and I wasted no time in getting away, barely reaching my all-terrain vehicle in time. If I had stood my ground though, I expect Buster would have backed off.

The experience serves to remind us that all wolves are not the same, that some may be aggressive on occasion, and that unpleasant encounters with them are always at least partially our fault. But considering the number of wolves in Minnesota, remarkably few wolf-human encounters have been reported. Most were pure chance, and neither the wolf nor the person generally stayed around long enough for anything bad to happen.

During the 1993 John Beargrease Sled Dog Marathon, a dogsled race from Duluth to Grand Portage and back, a dog team encountered a lone wolf on a remote stretch of the trail. One can only wonder why the wolf didn't take off running. When it saw the dozen or so dogs bearing down on it, the wolf simply froze, and the team ran right into it. The startled wolf offered no resistance and, after freeing itself from the dog team's leads, it began to run alongside the dogs as they resumed their race.

The racer handling the sled later quipped that he had considered hooking the big wolf up as part of the team. The rules of the race forbid adding dogs once the race has begun, he noted, but they say nothing about adding wolves.

Again, the story points to the unpredictability of wolves. Despite the fact that wolves have had thousands of chances to harm people—and have passed on those chances—they remain wild animals. The day may come when a young and foolish wolf will attack a person, probably mistaking him or her for some animal. That incident will not be sufficient reason to lapse into our old ways of thinking, or to punish all wolves by eradicating them—any more than it would make sense to get rid of all dogs because one dog bit a person. If we are to accept the wolf, we must accept all aspects of its nature.

There is a spiritual side to the wolf, as there is to every creature on this planet, but deifying an animal is a strange business. I suppose that, when we imbue the wolf with spiritual qualities, we're not behaving so differently from the aborigines who regarded the wolf as a totem animal from which they hoped to learn. But while the earlier totem seekers admired the spirit of the wolf, they remembered its reality. Though they honored the wolf and recognized it as another "people" of hunters sharing the same world, they also knew it as a flesh-and-blood creature—one that killed and ate other creatures, and one whose fur could warm the human being fortunate enough to possess it.

The farther people get from nature, the more they tend to misunderstand the natural world and its inhabitants. Somewhere in our primal roots, we still recognize something of ourselves in the wolf. We dimly remember that we, too, were once creatures of the woods and plains. We once lived much as wolves live, and though we now must struggle to understand this aspect of our spirit, the struggle is good. It has come none too soon for the health of the wolf and the survival of the planet.

Sigurd Olson died while snowshoeing in the winter of 1982. He was 83 years old.

From time to time, I stop in and visit his lovely wife, Elizabeth, at their home in Ely. Elizabeth Olson is a marvelous person. She shines, as if polished by the fire of life, by the blazing battles for the wilderness that her husband so valiantly fought.

If Sigurd was sometimes controversial in his own community, he needed only to travel as far away as Duluth before he would find himself regarded as a hero. For Sig, there were accolades. Elizabeth, however, had to go to church, had to attend PTA meetings, and had to shop at the market with neighbors who sometimes viciously disagreed with her husband's beliefs. Hers is great courage.

On my most recent visit, Elizabeth took me from the "public" part of the house—the living room where Sig's friends and admirers still gather—and invited me into a part of the house I'd never seen before. She had a gleam in

her eye and a wry smile, so I knew there was a purpose to her invitation.

We walked upstairs, then turned into a room. Elizabeth pointed at a wall. I turned to see, my eyes first taking in the length of what had been Sig's bed. On the wall, above the foot of the bed, hung a framed photograph.

It was a photograph of a wolf. Not only that, it was one of *my* photos, a photo I'd given Sig years before. In fact, it was the first good photo of a wolf I'd ever taken. A few years after I gave him the photo, he told me that he had hung it in a special place. I'd always assumed it was on display in his writing shack.

Elizabeth smiled radiantly. There wasn't much to say. I was speechless, and truly moved that Sig had appreciated the wolf so much. A thought occurred to me: Perhaps one of the reasons I've been so fortunate in photographing wolves and getting my work published is that I have had a guardian angel watching over me.

In many ways, Sig has been that angel.

There was a great satisfaction in knowing that the wolves were in the country, that it was wild enough and still big enough for them to roam and hunt. That night the wilderness of the Quetico-Superior was what the voyageurs had known two hundred years before, as primitive and unchanged as before discovery.

My earliest wolf photograph, a sig olson favorite.

Sigurd Olson reinforces that which is the magic of wolves: If a country is wild enough for wolves, then it is wild enough for the human spirit. If it is big enough for wolves, it is big enough to accommodate our primordial needs. Wolves make a country alive and complete, for without wolves (and in some places, grizzlies) the country becomes merely countryside, tamed because, though it may retain its beauty, it has lost its vitality. If predators do not stalk the hillsides, then the ancient pact has been violated, and the prey species must live as semi-domesticated animals. Without wolves and their wildness, the country lacks the very electricity of life. The thrill that Sigurd felt on that frozen night is exactly what separates existence from living.

I have seen wolves all of my life. Some were wolves of the mind, such as those I saw when I was a child dreaming of the north country, where wolves stalked through moonlit forests.

Others were wolves of my hopes, such as those I pursued without much success early in my photographic career. Others were the real thing—the wolves of Ellesmere Island in the Arctic and the wolves of Ravenwood.

My sense of the wolf is just that—my sense. It will be different for you and for each of us. But there are some things I know are a part of the mystery of wolves.

Wolves bring us in touch with our historic selves. Just as mental health depends upon accepting one's true self, so spiritual health depends upon

allowing that true self to flourish. Our society has sought to distance us from our primal ancestry, as if to deny that a half-naked hunter-gatherer lives in the human spirit. Even those who profess to love or admire wolves often deny their own primal nature, for they have great difficulty reconciling their love for animals with the knowledge that animals die, that creatures eat other creatures, and that humans, too, are predators.

We adopted the wolf, or the wolf adopted us, because the two of us are so very similar. That is very significant. Thousands of years ago, we brought a powerful, intelligent predator into our caves and our lodges, and today it sleeps at our feet. While we were learning to love the wolf that became the dog, we somehow learned to hate the wolf that stayed the wolf. I hope this will change. If we despise the wolf, we despise the true nature of the world in which we live. And our planet's health depends upon recognizing that we face the same biological constraints as the wolf and all other life.

Once, on assignment for *National Geographic*, I spent several days riding on a train while crossing northern China (which happens to be at exactly the same latitude as Ravenwood). One of my tasks was to photograph the Manchurian tiger and the red-crowned crane. When I explained this mission to my Chinese guides, their faces went blank. None of the people I spoke with could comprehend why anyone would want to visit or look at nature.

These people had no time to contemplate nature. They contemplated

THE MOST HAUNTING SOUNDS AT RAVENWOOD ARE PROVIDED BY THE LOON AND THE WOLF.

one hundred fifty

SEPTEMBER IS MY FAVORITE TIME IN CANOE COUNTRY.

SENSITIVE EARS REACT TO THE ECHO OF A DISTANT HOWL.

one hundred fifty-two

A STAND OF VIRGIN WHITE PINE.

one hundred fifty-three

survival. For them, nature was only something in the way. And as I traveled across the countryside, I saw no birds or other wildlife, nothing but manipulated landscapes filled with people and their works. Whenever I see that landscape in my mind, I pray that what I saw was not a foreshadowing of our planet's future.

In the last half century, we've begun to see wilderness as a tonic, as a thing necessary to our mental and ecological health. And in that wilderness the wolf still dwells. When the wilderness was feared, so was the wolf. Now that the wilderness is good, so is the wolf. And so, for better or worse, the wolf has been, and may always be, the symbol of wilderness.

When the white vastness of a wilderness lake is punctuated with wolf tracks, I do not stop to contemplate these things. I feel awed to be in a place where nature rules, and where the first rule of nature is the only rule of nature: Survive.

As I track the wolves, I am accompanied by an earlier me: I am the boy following foxes.

As I look across the frozen lake and see that the wolves have tested the wind below the hill, I become aware of a still earlier me: I am a man discovering the virgin world, wondering where the wolves are going and if by luck they might lead me to meat for my family.

As I follow the tracks to the south slope of the hill where the wolves made their beds in the sun, an even earlier me awakens: I am the aborigine who follows his wolf/dogs to the caribou he has wounded.

A WHITE CEDAR BOG CONCEALS MANY SECRETS.

And then I see that the wolves have loped off with their loose-jointed stride, vanishing into the cedars across the lake. They have rested, they are hungry, and so they have resumed their quest for food. That is what they want and need. There is no mystery to that. A wolf knows how to survive. Every molecule tells it how. A wolf knows how to make more wolves.

We must never forget that what the wolf wants, we want: food, space, peace, social order, and a healthy environment in which to live.

Of course, the wolf wants one more thing that should come as no surprise to any of us.

Brother Wolf wants to be left alone.

D ave Beers mourns the loss of an old friend. His old gray wolf is dead. He has kept his eye on her for several years, and every spring she has borne a litter of young wolves which have brought David a neat little sum in the way of bounties. There seems to have been some kind of an understanding between Mr. Beers and the old wolf. At any rate, they have worked together very harmoniously and David has taken good care of her. But a week or two ago, some wolf hunters who didn't seem to know about the partnership chanced to run across her in one of their crusades, and the hounds put an end to her career. As soon as Dave heard of it, he counted himself about $50 out.

This account of man and wolf appeared in 1893 in the *Rock County Star Herald*, my boyhood hometown newspaper, and the story touched me deeply. That I encountered it while working on this last section of the book seemed a remarkable coincidence. That it happened in an all-too-familiar locale seemed no less amazing.

Dave Beers' relationship with the she-wolf, which involved robbing her of her pups each year and turning them in for bounties, typifies our recent relationship with the wolf. My current hometown newspaper, the *Ely Echo*, recently ran an editorial titled "Better Than the Bounty." The newspaper acknowledged that the attitude of local citizens toward wolves was changing because these wonderful animals bring in tourists, and tourists bring dollars to the community. The editorial ends by saying: "There's packs of cash in the wolf packs." In the 100 years that have passed between the writing of these two newspaper accounts, not much has really changed. Wolves are apparently perceived by some to possess little or no intrinsic worth; they are only valuable for the cash they generate.

Something else stirred when I read the Beers account. He lived near my great-grandfather's prairie homestead, and the Beers' farm is owned today by a distant relative of mine. I wonder if my great-grandfather ever joined Beers or practiced similar bountying? I do know that the story of Beers and the wolf drove a point home to me in a way that nothing else has. The very spot where I grew up was once home to wolves but, unless humans disappear, never again will a she-wolf bear a litter of pups on the plains of my youth. There is a sadness to that knowledge.

As I finish this book, I realize that much of my career with wolves seemed preordained or, at the very least, remarkably fortuitous. If one event had changed, I might never have pursued the wolves of my dreams.

It was unreasonable for me to believe that I could walk down a forest trail just crossed by wolves and photograph them from 12 feet away. But I was in college, and I was young, and I thought I could, and so I did one frozen Minnesota morning. I left my truck and crept toward the spot where I'd last seen the wolves. Despite my attempt at stealth, the wolves surely heard or saw me coming. Yet they waited. That unlikely, successful encounter inspired me to continue. Years later, when a ghostly arctic wolf pack materialized unexpectedly from the ice-fog of Ellesmere Island and tolerated my presence, I knew that I must return and tell the story of those wolves. Always, something drew me on.

I never intended to be known as a wolf photographer. These years of study haven't just been about consorting with wolves. Telling their story became important. And, as is the case with much of my other photography, I realize now that I was trying to recapture something we've lost. It has been my fate to encounter wolves, and with that fate has come the opportunity to help ensure the wolf's survival.

But there may be more than fate at work. When we long ago adopted the wolf, we were able to do so because these animals were intelligent enough to benefit from the joining. Recently, animal behaviorists have begun to speculate that some of the more intelligent animals possess the ability to think. While they've mostly limited their research to socially complex primates, I find striking confirmations in my experiences with wolves. These researchers believe that humans—and perhaps other social animals—have evolved the ability to think as survival strategy. A creature that can anticipate a rival's moves or a partner's actions can capitalize on that knowledge by avoiding unpleasant events or partaking in pleasant ones.

One of the benchmarks in determining this ability, which can be equated with the sense of self, is the propensity of an animal to deceive another for its own benefit. Humans are experts at this sort of deception. So are chimpanzees, according to the research. In repeated tests, chimpanzees put their own interests first by hiding food, or by forming political partnerships in order to please the clan leader. In my experience, loyalty within the wolf pack is often more consistent than loyalty within the family of man. I might add that the politics of wolf preservation and the science of studying wolves is more vicious and complicated than any wolf pack I've had the pleasure of studying.

I have witnessed wolves that would not cache food when other wolves were around; nor would they bury it if they thought I was watching. Yet once they believed they were alone, they stashed their treasure. Like the chimpanzee, the wolf at times seems self-conscious.

Two social carnivores, humans and wolves, formed a pact. We brought to the partnership our large brain with its demands for greater quantities of high-calorie food. The wolf contributed its ability to secure the most concentrated of all foods: meat. Did that first union with another species lead to human physiological changes made possible by having a more dependable food supply? Did it perhaps even lead to an increase in intellect?

The great love we feel for our dogs, a love that leads people to risk their lives for their pet (which I have done on at least one occasion), is perhaps a reflection of that early pact between our species. Even the wild wolf seems to have kept some implied promise, for the wolf is the only large predator that does not attack humans. Despite the benefits we've reaped from this pairing, we deal wolves mostly death, instead of the respect they deserve.

One winter night, after emerging into the glacial Minnesota air following a long and hot interlude in my log sauna, I lay *au naturel* in the snow near the foot of a frozen waterfall. There, I made a snow angel as I steamed and cooled beneath the northern lights.

The next morning, I walked to the cliff above the angel. Looking down, I saw that a wolf's tracks wandered from the forest onto the ice, bisecting my angel as they crossed the snow-covered, frozen pond.

I was moved by the symbolism. Like ghosts in the night, the wolf and I had occupied the very same space. I realized then that we are *all* occupying the wolf's space, though we're no longer likely to share space like the farms owned by Dave Beers and my great-grandfather.

If the wolf is to survive, we must pay our debt. Let us hope that, at Ravenwood and other wild places, we find it within ourselves to share again, as we did for millennia, to ensure that the wolf will forever have its space.

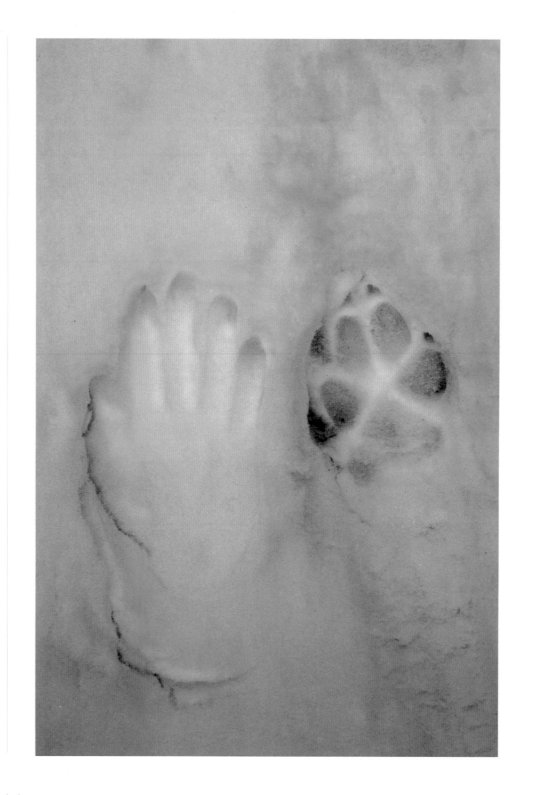

Lake

Canada

United States

Bald Eagle nest

x 1100 Year old
Cedar tree

Camp

x Camp

Lake

Loon nest

Portage Creek

Wilderness

Birch Forest

N

B.W.C.A.W.

Raven
Nest
x

Canoe Route

Camp

Winter

Portage
Trail

Wolf pack encounter

Lake

Winter

Bo

Cliff

Orchid
Bog

Bear
scrat
tree

Water fall

Dead bear

Black
Ducks

Moose

Wolf pack

Chase deer
on ice

Lake